About Demos

Who we are

Demos is the think tank for everyday democracy. We believe everyone should be able to make personal choices in their daily lives that contribute to the common good. Our aim is to put this democratic idea into practice by working with organisations in ways that make them more effective and legitimate.

What we work on

We focus on six areas: public services; science and technology; cities and public space; people and communities; arts and culture; and global security.

Who we work with

Our partners include policy-makers, companies, public service providers and social entrepreneurs. Demos is not linked to any party but we work with politicians across political divides. Our international network – which extends across Eastern Europe, Scandinavia, Australia, Brazil, India and China – provides a global perspective and enables us to work across borders.

How we work

Demos knows the importance of learning from experience. We test and improve our ideas in practice by working with people who can make change happen. Our collaborative approach means that our partners share in the creation and ownership of new ideas.

What we offer

We analyse social and political change, which we connect to innovation and learning in organisations. We help our partners show thought leadership and respond to emerging policy challenges.

How we communicate

As an independent voice, we can create debates that lead to real change. We use the media, public events, workshops and publications to communicate our ideas. All our books can be downloaded free from the Demos website.

www.demos.co.uk

First published in 2006
© Demos
Some rights reserved – see copyright licence for details

ISBN 1 84180 160 7
Copy edited by Julie Pickard, London
Typeset by utimestwo, Collingtree, Northamptonshire
Printed by Upstream, London

For further information and
subscription details please contact:

Demos
Magdalen House
136 Tooley Street
London SE1 2TU

telephone: 0845 458 5949
email: hello@demos.co.uk
web: www.demos.co.uk

Working Progress
How to reconnect young people and organisations

Sarah Gillinson
Duncan O'Leary

DEM⊙S

DEM⊚S

Contents

Acknowledgements

Particular thanks go to Steve Aumayer, Tom Glover and Alistair MacLeod at Orange for making this project possible. Thanks also to Paul Miller and Eddie Gibb for their roles in setting up the project early on.

From Demos, thanks to all the interns who helped support the project – Noel Hatch and James Huckle for their research support and to all those who helped with the final event. Thanks also to Alison Harvie for project management. As always, thanks to Julia Huber for seeing the pamphlet through to publication, to Simon Parker and Sam Hinton-Smith for their insights throughout and to Tom Bentley for helping us to sharpen and clarify the final argument.

Finally, thanks to all those who talked with us about their thoughts and experiences during the research. We also greatly appreciate the time spared by polling and focus group participants to be interviewed.

As ever, all errors and omissions remain our own.

Sarah Gillinson
Duncan O'Leary
June 2006

Foreword

Alastair MacLeod

Like you, I know that change is a fact of modern life. And when you consider the fast-paced rate of change as it is applied to modern business, it is hardly surprising that we are witnessing a worrying disconnect between the needs and expectations of employers and employees. This is particularly evident when you look at young people entering organisations for the first time from the more, and very differently, structured world of education. Is it really possible to prepare the next generation for successful careers in the workplace when the parameters are constantly and so radically changing?

Orange believes that by working with Demos, we have generated practical steps and suggestions that could start to reconnect and mobilise these dynamic forces. Their ultimate aim is to help employers, government and young people engage in more useful dialogue that recognises their collective ability to shape a brighter future for all parties.

'Reconnection' is a challenge for all organisations, including Orange, as we refine our recruitment strategy and staff development programmes. This report highlights a world in flux – available jobs, the skills and knowledge required, the nature of organisations and employees themselves are all changing. We need to develop a better understanding of the new skills that recruits will need and the roles we are actually recruiting for. Gone are the days when graduates were simply recruited for old-style leadership roles.

This report focuses on young people and their experiences of organisations, but we should not forget that the ageing workforce and the pressures faced by working parents add to this complicated employment picture. Orange itself is committed to being more flexible in order to retain the skills and knowledge of older workers and parents. In short, governments, employers and workers all need to be aware of and react to significant changes to working practices and expectations to ensure the future success of British business.

UK plc has long since moved from manufacturing to a service-led economy. However, it is increasingly apparent that in the global economy, human talent will be the key factor in ensuring the continued dominance of British business. It is for this reason that human resources directors rated creativity and innovation as the most important graduate skills in ten years' time. Imagination will help organisations secure competitive advantage in the future and it is up to us to ensure we have created the right environment for people with that 'x-factor' to develop and flourish.

At the same time, building on findings from *Disorganisation*, the previous Orange and Demos report, we know that employees with these talents are demanding that organisations 'loosen up', offer more flexibility and a work environment that is more aligned with their personal values. The Orange Future Enterprise Coalition has also identified work–life balance as a vital skill for the modern workplace. It sees an important role for organisations in helping to inspire young people to get the most out of their relationships and the world around them. In today's world, this includes the ability to use new technologies to your own advantage rather than letting them impose or dictate a particular way of life.

Converged technologies that result from the coming together of the mobile, fixed and internet worlds have the potential to help marry this need for ever greater organisational efficiency or hyper-organisation with the flexibility needed to create an environment in which young people can be engaged, motivated and creative.

For Orange, that news is positive. We see a new generation of employees emerging: a generation that understands how best to use mobile technology and how to derive maximum benefit for both their professional and personal lives. Polling for *Working Progress* demonstrates this point, with 43 per cent of graduates reporting that technology has made it 'easier' to maintain work–life balance, compared with 19 per cent who felt it had made maintaining a balance harder.

As this generation rises through the workplace, we will see a gradual change in the way businesses operate, with a mental 'switching off' replacing the physical 'leaving work' at the end of the day.

This 'switching off' is the boundary between work and home life. When employees are 'off', they are inaccessible to their employer, and personally responsible for their actions – an email sent from the employee's mobile device when 'off', for example, is not attributable to the organisation, but to the individual. When employees are 'on', however, they are expected to communicate about work-related matters only and any use of a mobile service would be associated with the organisation, not the individual.

This is just one adjustment in a time of profound and long-lasting change. One of the few certainties is that identifying a long-term strategy to help us reconnect young people and organisations successfully depends on building real dialogue and better relationships between employees, employers and government. We hope that some of the recommendations featured in this report help begin that process.

Ultimately, though, progress will not be made if individuals do not take responsibility for their own learning, career and life choices. Young people will continue to drive change, but they then must ensure they grasp the opportunities open to them with both hands.

Alastair MacLeod is Vice President, Orange Business Services UK.

About this report

Working Progress is based on a combination of literature-based and qualitative research undertaken between December 2005 and April 2006.

We undertook over 30 interviews with employers, human resources (HR) professionals, graduates and training providers as well as holding three focus groups in London, Coventry and Cheshire with young people who graduated from university in the past one to three years.

GfK NOP also undertook two polls on our behalf during March and April 2006. The first of these questioned 539 graduates about their experiences of entering the workplace. The second interviewed 50 HR directors or the most senior professional in charge of graduate recruitment in FTSE 200 companies or equivalent.

1. Introduction

The stories are familiar: graduates failing to live up to employers' expectations; young people feeling disappointed and downtrodden by life after university; the education system trying to bridge the gap. Despite rising academic attainment, somehow the traditional 21-year cycle of learning and preparation for the world of work is not quite preparing people for the reality of life in modern organisations – resulting in lower productivity for business and frustrating false starts for young people.

This pamphlet aims to develop a better understanding of this problem by starting with the experiences of young people entering organisations. Drawing on their own perspective and that of employers through original survey work, it asks what can be done to help them survive and succeed in the workplaces of the future.

We argue that there is a damaging disconnect between young people and organisations – a disconnect between the training of today and the workplaces of tomorrow, and between the changing values of young people and the organisational cultures that they encounter.

At the heart of this disconnect is a lack of understanding on both sides of the other's needs. The survey work carried out for this report shows that employers appreciate that graduates are more than skilled than a decade ago, but that at the same time 54 per cent of HR directors say they find it increasingly difficult to find the right graduates with the right skills.

The answer to this apparent paradox lies in a lack of 'soft' skills: employers want communication skills and think creativity is vital for the future – but a third of graduates feel awkward in meetings and they rank creativity as only the eighth most important skill for the future. Most worrying of all – *graduates don't seem to be aware of the problem*. Over 90 per cent of them think they are well prepared for the world of work.

But employers are also suffering from a disconnect. While 88 per cent of British employees believe that it is important that the organisation they work for is committed to living its values, only 45 per cent believe their employer does.[1] Graduates used to working in the peer-to-peer environment of university find it hard to shift to organisational hierarchies and difficult to relate to their bosses. They find it hard to balance the pressures of work and life outside the office in the hierarchical new world they have just entered.

These disconnects have emerged because of a series of rapid shifts in both the *supply* of jobs available from employers and the *demand* for jobs, or expectations of employment, on the part of graduates. On the supply side, the jobs available in the economy are changing, as is the nature of many organisations themselves. In our own GfK NOP poll, HR directors rated creativity and innovation as the most important graduate skills in ten years' time. On the demand side, the expectations and values of young people are shifting, alongside the changing nature of the graduate career itself.

We suggest that these changes mean new challenges for employees, which increase the importance of 'intangible' personal qualities, such as the ability to work in a team or to be creative. And we argue that they provide new questions for employers, as they struggle to find ways to attract, motivate and support a generation of young people with higher debt, different values and more demanding jobs than ever before.

In this environment, we must find new and different opportunities to develop the talents of young people, which do not fall into the neat categories of educational 'standards' or vocational learning. Acquiring vocational skills, or achieving high levels of literacy and numeracy, is important, but learning how to *make use of these skills* within an organisation is equally important.

To do this, we will need to get beyond the process of batting blame back and forth between employers, government and young people – and start to forge more useful conversations and partnerships involving change and effort from all three.

This is not an argument that education should be reduced to a conveyer belt, which simply 'delivers' young people to organisations with the right skills. As Ken Robinson argues, the first 18 years of our life are more than a rehearsal.[2] But giving young people the opportunity to apply their learning beyond conventional settings, in creative and expressive ways, connecting to real-life issues, points to a richer experience of learning, rather than a narrower one.

Neither should a new approach signal a content-free curriculum, concerned solely with working in teams or role playing at office life. As our working lives become more complex, we do require an ever-growing set of capacities, but these skills and aptitudes cannot be developed in isolation from content and knowledge. As Tom Bentley makes clear: 'It is impossible to develop or demonstrate emotional intelligence in the absence of some other question or issue. One cannot work in a team for its own sake.'[3]

Last, a call for more human and responsive organisations is not an argument that seeks to pit the interests of employees against those of organisations. We argue that for young people to be engaged, motivated and creative – as employers would wish – their work environment must be one where they feel genuinely at home. This points to approaches that go beyond standard work–life balance policies, or simply paying more to paper over the cracks.

In short, we argue that for education and training to genuinely prepare young people for organisational life, it must support wider forms of personal development; and for organisations to benefit from these skills and capacities – and to fulfil their duty of care towards young people – they must create working environments that are aligned to young people's values and which provide genuine support when it is needed.

Our research has focused on graduates entering the workplace, but we would suggest that there are lessons that apply to those who have not attended university as much as to those who have. We have also deliberately looked beyond conventional settings and formal education and training in order to pick up some clues as to what a new approach might look like.

In the following chapter we discuss some of the ways in which the jobs that young people enter into after university are changing – due to shifts in both the supply and demand for jobs. In chapter 3 we examine the response to these changes so far from government and organisations themselves, and highlight the disconnect between employers and young people that still persists.

In chapter 4 we explore why these changes have failed to bridge the gap between employers and graduates, as we identify an important set of broadly personal capacities that appear to be of growing importance inside organisations. Chapter 5 outlines some of the ways that government, the education system and other organisations could support the wider development of young people, and argues for a much richer range of opportunities and experiences for young people during their formal education.

Chapter 6 explores the expectations and experiences of young people when they finally reach organisations. It argues that the disconnect that we identify has important implications for organisations themselves. We suggest that organisations must move beyond conventional policies if they are to support young people in fulfilling and productive jobs.

Finally, to help address this disconnect between young people and organisations, we make the following recommendations – each of which is explored further in the concluding chapter.

1 **The government should introduce a Skills Portfolio, to help capture some of the learning, skills and aptitudes that are often not reflected in traditional qualifications.**

2 **Schools should hold termly equivalents of 'parents'**

evenings' for local businesses and community organisations.

3   The government should support the introduction of an Investors in Community accreditation for businesses.

4   Universities should draw on the work being done at universities like Glasgow Caledonian University and MIT-Cambridge to embed transferable, work-based skills into the curriculum.

5   Companies should hold entrance interviews and skills audits for young people entering their organisations.

6   Companies should recognise work–life balance as a set of skills as well as a set of legal obligations or company policy.

7   Companies should learn from leading practice and provide 'deep support' for young people entering organisations.

8   Employers should work with each other, and with young people, to develop an online, open-access training resource that young people can consult when they need to, to supplement their own development.

9   Organisations should find ways to support the peer-to-peer networks, both inside and outside their walls, that young people rely on and value so highly when they enter organisations.

10   Companies should consider organising themselves into networks, offering short-term 'skills development' contracts for new graduates, involving placements in a number of different companies or institutions.

2. It's the knowledge economy, stupid

The world of work is awash with change. Companies have been downsized, outsourced, re-imagined and re-engineered. The countervailing forces of efficiency and innovation drive new approaches to management. Technology helps organisations become simultaneously more connected and more dispersed. Global competition sees whole countries searching for their comparative advantage. Company assets walk in and out of the door each day. Patterns of work have changed, as has the profile of the workforce itself, with a more discerning generation of consumers entering the market for jobs.

From the perspective of an employer hiring a new graduate, these shifts can be understood as changes both to the *supply* of jobs provided by organisations and to the *demands* of young people themselves entering the workforce.

On the supply side, there are two key factors driving an ongoing process of change:

O   The economy is restructuring.
O   Expectations on employees are growing.

But while young people entering organisations are *subject* to two powerful forces that are shaping their opportunities and experiences in the workplace, they are also *driving change* themselves.

Two trends stand out in particular:

O   Organisations are under pressure to 'loosen up'.
O   Working patterns are changing – as we work more flexibly
    and do many more jobs than was previously the case.

The economy is restructuring

Perhaps the most obvious driver of change in the jobs that young
people do is the structure of the economy itself. The Chancellor has
argued that:

> At no point since the industrial revolution has the restructuring
> of global economic activity been so dramatic; at no point has
> there been such a shift in production . . . and at no point in our
> whole history has the speed and scale of technological change
> been so fast and pervasive.[4]

The evidence certainly points to sizeable shifts in the types of jobs
that are – and will increasingly be – available to young people.
Research commissioned by the Department for Education and Skills
demonstrates the structural shift taking place. As figure 1 illustrates,
the elementary occupations, administrative and clerical jobs of the
old economy are on the wane, while the forecasters predict that
Britain will continue to need more professionals, associate
professionals and managers in the future.

Although there are nuances that these statistics do not illustrate,[5]
the long-term picture is clear – competition from abroad and
technological advances at home mean that the types of jobs that
young people can expect in the future are going through a significant
period of change. In many jobs, we must demonstrate our
comparative advantage not just over others in the UK, but also over
potential employees from around the world.

As Philip Brown and Hugh Lauder put it: 'There are no longer
British, German, or American jobs, just British, German and
American workers.'[6] The voice on the end of the phone is just as likely
to be in Bangalore as it is in Barnet, while the four million graduates

Figure 1. Restructuring of the British economy

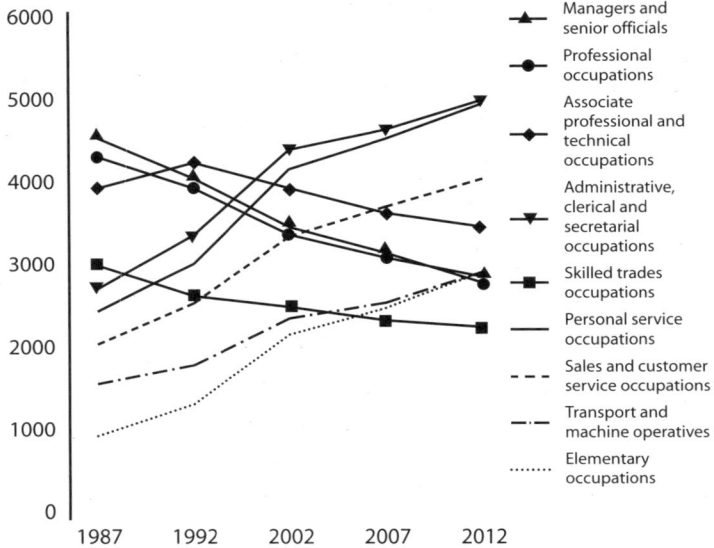

Source: DfES, *Working Futures*, National Report 2003/04 (Warwick: Institute for Employment Research, 2004).

produced by China and India each year are beginning to fashion 'a new geography of science'. India may have graduates working in call centres, but it also represents a new breed of innovation superpowers emerging in the East.[7]

In this environment, good people and their skills are one of the most important advantages companies and countries can possess – research for HM Treasury shows that human and physical capital account for the entire productivity gap between Britain and almost all other competitor countries.[8]

Technological progress compounds and accelerates this shift. In broad terms, advances in technology are helping the smart become smarter, as traditionally low-skilled jobs gradually wither away. The analyst benefits from faster processing and more options, while factory workers are replaced by mechanised production lines, bank clerks by cash machines, and administrators by knowledge management tools.

This trend – that 'things will increasingly be made by things'[9] – is described by Frank Levy and Richard Murname as a 'new division of labour' between humans and machines. They argue: 'Computers' comparative advantage over people lies in tasks that can be described using rules-based logic: step-by-step procedures with an action specified for every contingency.'[10]

In one sense, this provides a daunting picture of human jobs replaced by intelligence embedded in machinery, but in another it reveals the comparative advantage that people will continue to hold – the ability to adapt to new situations, to engage with others, to solve unexpected problems, to generate new ideas and identify new opportunities.

Our own GfK NOP survey of HR directors of FTSE 200 companies (or equivalent) clearly demonstrated this trend. When asked what the most important skills and qualities will be for graduates in ten years' time they collectively ranked 'creativity and innovation' highest – above literacy, numeracy, IT capability, communication skills, problem-solving and multitasking (see table 1).

As Gordon Brown himself has said, by 2020, health, education and the creative industries will be our greatest exports.[11] In the report that it delivered to the Chancellor last year, the Cox Review of Creativity in Business concluded that the UK has a 'window of opportunity' of between five and ten years to develop the kind of creative skills that will be necessary to compete in a global economy.[12]

In his book *The Rise of the Creative Class*,[13] Richard Florida offers an explanation as to why this is the case. He asks:

What powers economic growth? It's not technology – technology is a raw material. What makes human beings unique is one thing – creativity. All else are subsets. Creativity powers economic growth.

Table 1. *HR directors*: Which do you believe will be the most important skill, quality or aptitude for potential graduate employees to have in ten years' time?

Creativity and innovation	24%
Flexibility and multitasking	20%
Communication/communicating ideas	18%
Problem-solving	10%

Source: GfK NOP polling

These shifts, then, have profound implications for the opportunities for – and expectations of – young graduates entering the workplace.

Expectations on employees are growing

A second major driver of change in the working lives of young people is the growing level of expectation that those entering organisations are expected to meet. Our survey evidence underlined the fact that jobs are becoming more demanding and complex across the economy: fully 80 per cent of the companies questioned believe that the demands placed on graduates have grown over the last ten years.

The dream employee of the past might have been someone who was superb at understanding and implementing established processes and practices to meet the demands of a hierarchically delivered decision.

Today, having invested in human capital, organisations generally want to benefit from it – creating flatter, more networked organisations and giving employees more responsibility for interactions with customers, producing innovation and delivering service improvements. In our GfK NOP survey, when employers were asked which personal attributes they looked for the most in potential graduate employees, only 8 per cent responded with 'responsiveness to requests'.

What people know is important, but so too is how they might respond in any number of situations, many of which cannot be anticipated. Adaptability, improvisation and bluffing are all becoming key skills. One recent graduate commented:

> *If I could give one piece of advice? You've got to be able to bulls**t!*

Large hierarchies, with decisions made exclusively at the top of the pyramid, are slowly being replaced by more networked organisational structures. As Tom Bentley has argued, organisations are increasingly likely to store knowledge in *people* through training and development, rather than by imposing rules or procedures.[14]

The words of Tim Smit, the managing director of the Eden Project in Cornwall, on the eve of the project's launch, perhaps exemplify this shift. Addressing his employees, he told them: 'Tomorrow people will ask you for things, or to do things that we haven't yet thought of. If you respond in a way in which things go wrong, no-one will blame you. If you do nothing, I'll sack you.'[15] In their discussion of life skills and social exclusion, Hannah Lownsbrough argues that 'how an employee might respond in a given situation has become more important than what s/he already knows',[16] indicating that this trend may reach well beyond the world of graduate employment. Increasingly, it seems, employees need initiative as well as intelligence, creativity as well as qualifications.

In response to this, 'leadership' is increasingly understood as an activity, rather than a position within an organisation.[17] If the survey evidence is to be believed, the language and practice of innovation are becoming democratised in many workplaces. Recent studies have shown that:

○ 33 per cent of business leaders expect their organisations to become less hierarchical in the future, compared with only 25 per cent who think they will become more hierarchical[18]

○ 67 per cent of companies now report that they train

managers to identify and develop new ideas, compared
with 20 per cent in 2002

o employers rank having a workforce able to identify,
develop and adopt new ideas is second only to 'the right
ideas at the right time' as important factors underpinning
innovation

o only two in five companies (41%) agree that
investment in R&D is the best indicator of innovation
activity.[19]

This search for workable new ideas becomes ever more important in
an age where product life-cycles shorten, and new technology helps to
constantly drive and support change. It is a startling statistic that it
took nearly 40 years for 50 million people to own a radio, 16 years for
50 million people to own a personal computer, and just five years for
50 million people to connect to the internet.[20] Just eight years ago
only 10 per cent of people in Britain had mobile phones.[21]

In this context, many leading companies are deciding that
innovation is too important to be left to a few people with 'manager'
in their job title. Toyota famously allows any employee to stop the
production line if they have an idea about how to improve the system.
The company 3M, living up to its motto of 'spirit of innovation',
allows employees to take up to 15 per cent of their work time to
pursue 'any idea that they want to work on which is not part of their
job expectation' – using company resources to do so.[22] Few
companies have gone as far as Ricardo Semler's Semco in Brazil,[23] but
those that have found the right combination of democratic
management and organisational coherence are reaping the rewards.
3M was judged by business leaders to be the most innovative in the
world in 2004, coming second only to Apple in 2005.[24]

To add to this constant quest for new ideas, there is the growing
complexity of many roles within organisations. We now expect
doctors to treat the illnesses as well as the patient. We still expect
teachers to deliver excellent lessons – but also to form relationships
with social workers, healthcare professionals, police, parents and the

wider community. Where knowledge of information and communication technology (ICT) used to be a niche area of expertise in
organisations, it is increasingly just another part of our daily routines.
The changing role of an engineer at Yorkshire Water, described in
the following case study, is emblematic of these changes.

Case study: Yorkshire Water

In 1995 Yorkshire Water faced a series of challenges. Confronted
with a demanding set of targets set by its regulator (the company
is a regional monopoly), the company set itself the challenge of
reducing its costs by £100 million, while improving service to its
customers.

To drive this process, the company set out to re-engineer its
business processes, fundamentally altering its relationship with
customers, and revolutionising the roles and responsibilities of
those working in the company.

Company engineers were given new technology. All engineers
were given laptops, complete with GPRS (mobile data transfer)
systems allowing them to access real-time information away from
the office. Rather than make continual trips to and from head
offices, engineers would now access and add to their own work
routines remotely.

Engineers were also given new responsibilities: to add to their
new self-directing role and their traditional set of technical responsibilities, they would be empowered to make commitments to
customers – and ensure those commitments were met through
tracking orders within the company and ensuring follow-up action.

Alan Harrison, managing director of Yorkshire Water's customer
management business, says that the process, which helped to save
well in excess of the £100 million target, was 'to allow the people
doing the real work to support themselves'. The new technology
was a significant step towards this – 'the only technology they'd
been given before was a shovel', he says – helping to transform the
role of the engineer from blue-collar worker to the mobile,

empowered and technologically enabled champion of the customer. 'Now he's not bottom of the pile,' says Harrison, 'he's the hero.'

Organisations are under pressure to 'loosen up'

It would be wrong to suggest that people have never cared about their overall experience of work, but, increasingly, we expect far more than just a wage from our employers. Research by Demos has highlighted a growing imperative for companies to 'loosen up' in order to recruit and retain the most talented staff. Paul Miller and Paul Skidmore argue that:

> Employees want more human organisations with greater autonomy and flexibility. They want an experience of work that is aligned with their values. They want a workplace forged in the image of their identities, not a workplace that tries to define them. They want organisations that can let go, and grant them a greater say in how things are run.[25]

This represents an opportunity for employers looking for more interesting, driven and multidimensional graduates, but also a possible threat to those who are not nimble enough to respond. Common Purpose, the leadership development and training organisation, has identified what it describes as a 'quarter life crisis', during which young, successful employees are likely to leave their pressurised jobs to embark on a search for meaning and personal expression through their work.[26]

This reflects what may be a broader shift in values across society. Research by MORI shows that the ways in which we judge companies is shifting dramatically. As figure 2 illustrates, the relative value we place, as consumers, on 'quality of products' has fallen significantly in the last 20 years, while the importance we place on honesty, integrity and treatment of staff have all grown.[27]

Figure 2. The changing way we judge companies

Q. What do you think are the most important things to know about a company in order to judge its reputation?

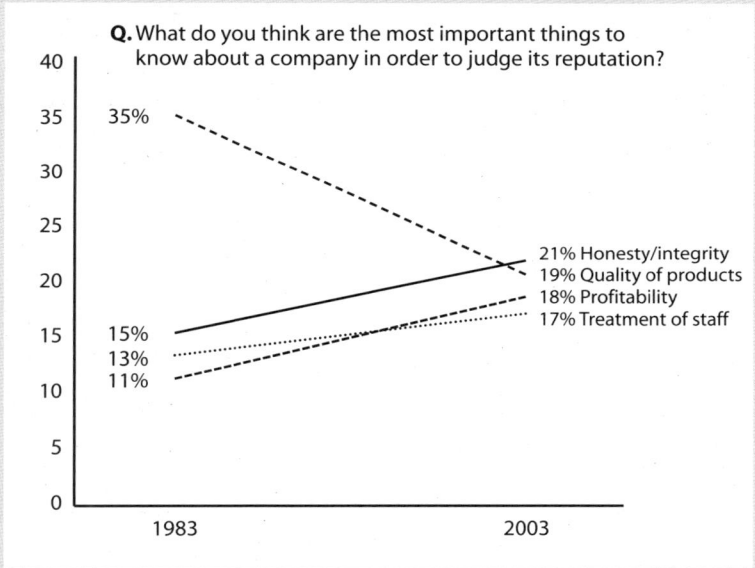

Base c. 2000 adults aged 16+
Source: MORI

Similarly, research carried out by Business in the Community has found that while 88 per cent of British employees believe that it is important that the organisation they work for is committed to living its values, only 45 per cent believe their employer does.[28]

Such trends have not gone unnoticed by the business world. The business consultants McKinsey have steadfastly been arguing for a shift in corporate values over the last year, making the case that social issues are taking on increasingly *strategic* importance for businesses as they seek to build much more meaningful relationships with their customers and employees.[29]

In their book, *The Support Economy*,[30] Zuboff and Maxmin argue that a changing economic paradigm offers a powerful explanation as to why this should be so. They suggest that we are in the process of moving from the 'mass economy' stimulated by Ford, and his revolutionary insight into mass production, to the support economy. This is an economy that is populated by individuals with far greater awareness of their own interests and needs, whose growing expectations of more tailored services are making traditional forms of organisations and ways of responding to customers defunct.

Zuboff and Maxmin predict that the most successful companies will be those that build services around the complexity of the market and the messiness of people's daily lives. Goods, products or services, they argue, will increasingly revolve around the needs of individuals, with companies pulling together highly personalised packages of support. In this context, the divide between our expectations as consumers and as employees is likely to blur. We will look to employers to sustain a more human experience in the workplace as well as in the market place.

So at a time when the number of adults in the working population is expected to fall for the first time since 1945,[31] it may be that the balance of power between employees and employers is beginning to shift in some areas of work. In some jobs, at least, it looks increasingly credible that young graduates will be able to take their values with them to the workplace as well as the ballot box and the high street.

Working patterns are changing

Finally, our patterns of work are changing – from our day-to-day working lives to the very structures of our careers. We change jobs more quickly, we carry them out more flexibly and we mix work and life in new ways.

In part, this is about formal hours worked – the nine-to-five working day lives on, but for fewer and fewer of us. As table 2, drawn from the *Labour Force Survey* in 2003, shows, one in five of us is now involved in some form of flexible working.

Increasingly, these new working patterns are enabled by technology. A job for a company in London can mean teleworking from Bristol.

Table 2. Employees with flexible working patterns[a], 2003[b] (percentages)

United Kingdom	Males	Females	All employees
Full-time employees			
Flexible working hours	9.7	14.9	11.6
Annualised working hours	4.9	5.1	5.0
Four and a half day week	1.8	1.1	1.5
Term-time working	1.2	5.8	2.9
Nine-day fortnight	0.4	0.3	0.3
Any flexible working pattern[c]	18.0	26.7	21.1
Part-time employees			
Flexible working hours	6.6	8.4	8.0
Annualised working hours	3.4	4.2	4.0
Term-time working	3.9	11.2	9.8
Job sharing	1.2	3.5	3.1
Any flexible working pattern[c]	16.9	26.7	24.8

[a] Percentages are based on totals that exclude people who did not state whether or not they had a flexible working arrangement. Respondents could give more than one answer.
[b] In spring. Data are not seasonally adjusted and have not been adjusted to take account of the Census 2001 results. See *Labour Force Survey* Appendix, Part 4: LFS reweighting.
[c] Includes other categories of flexible working not separately identified.
Source: Office for National Statistics, *Labour Force Survey* 2003

This shift brings with it a plethora of implications for both employees and employers. We must learn to 'manage' those who no longer sit in the same room with us every day, while organisations must also find ways to maintain company cultures when employees may well be spread in far-flung locations.

For employees, new technology provides exciting potential for improving the work–life balance – we can read emails on the train home, rather than sitting at a desk in the office. But we can access the

Table 3. Graduates: With regard to your working career, where do you expect to be in five years' time?

In the same career, but at a different company	42
In the same company	25
Running my own business	13
In a different career	8
Travelling	5
Not working, eg retired, housewife or househusband	1
Other	1
Don't know	5

Source: GfK NOP polling

server at work from our front rooms – at any time day or night. This points to the importance of companies and employees working together to find ways to take advantage of new technology and the potential for flexible working, in order to resolve the tension between what has been described as 'hyperoganisation' and 'disorganisation'.[32]

Further to this, while our experiences of *individual* jobs are changing, the breadth and variety of our *careers* continues to grow. At present, British workers change their jobs more often than any others in Europe,[33] while City & Guilds estimates that the average person starting their working life in 2025 will face 19 job changes compared with 13 for those starting out today.[34] These trends highlight the range of intellectual challenges and working environments that young people can expect to experience – and will need to adapt to – in a life's work. In our own GfK NOP survey, only one in four graduates expected to be in the same company in five years' time (see table 3).

These forces add up cumulatively to a fundamentally new set of challenges for young graduates entering organisations, and a new set of questions for organisations themselves. They are of course broad trends, none of which apply to every young person in every job. For example, previous research by Demos has found that companies are under pressure to 'hyperorganise' in the name of efficiency as much as they are to 'disorganise' in the spirit of innovation and human values.[35] New technology can mean more control for employers just as easily as it can signal more freedom for employees.[36] Nevertheless, these shifts pose a fascinating set of questions about the ability of young people to survive and thrive in the workplaces of the twenty-first century – and for their organisations to support and motivate them.

These questions have not gone unnoticed. The next chapter examines the response from government and from companies to the rising demands placed on young people entering organisations.

3. Education, education, education

Education is the best economic policy we have.

Tony Blair

Improving quality and standards in schools is, for me, both a political and personal obsession.

David Cameron

Raising standards is no good if they're the wrong standards.

Ken Robinson[37]

The rising demands that young people – and in particular graduates – face on entering organisations have certainly not gone unnoticed either by government or by companies themselves. The argument that we may have too many qualified people – that 'if everyone stands on their toes, no one sees any better'[38] – has rightly been dismissed.

The analogy ignores the effects of the technological progress discussed in the last chapter, and the fact that other nations and companies may all be standing on *their* toes, climbing up ladders, or perhaps building cranes to get a better view. In fact, this report shows that standing on our toes *may not be enough*.

Studies consistently highlight the importance of skills in sustaining business success and overcoming social exclusion. The Department for Education and Skills forecasts that by 2012 two-thirds of all jobs are expected to require qualifications at the equivalent of three A-levels or higher.[39] International comparisons see rising skill levels in Europe, America and in the East, pointing towards the 'high-skilled, high-wage' economy that is the aspiration of most developed economies in the twenty-first century.[40]

The importance of qualifications for young people entering the workforce is underlined by some striking statistics. On average, those with a degree are paid around 25 per cent more than those without; those with A-levels are paid around 15 per cent more than those without.[41] The figures are even more striking for basic literacy and numeracy. Only half of those people with no qualifications are in work, compared with 90 per cent of adults qualified to degree level – an important statistic, considering that over five million people of working age in the UK have no qualification at all, and one in six adults do not have the literacy skills expected of an 11-year-old.[42]

As a response to this challenge, government now spends around 5.3 per cent of GDP on education,[43] with education and skills as an expressed first priority. Ambitious targets have been established, aimed at raising participation in education and training from 16 onwards, with many more young people going to university.

And the signs are that this level of urgency, matched by record levels of investment, is having an impact. Figure 3 shows there has been a consistent rise in achievement at GCSE level in recent years, while, over the last decade, the proportion of the population with a degree has increased from one-fifth to over one-quarter of the population.[44]

The evidence is that organisations themselves recognise and value rising skill levels among young people. KPMG's 'Competitive Alternatives Report' in 2002[45] found that the availability of skilled labour ranked above all other factors – including transport infrastructure, tax exemptions and energy availability – as the most important factor in determining the location of inward investment.

Figure 3. Rising achievement at GCSE level (percentage of 15-year-olds achieving 5+ A*–C grades)

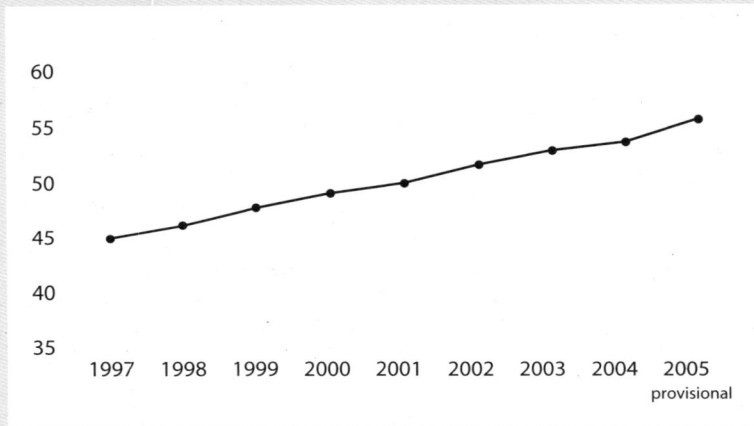

Source: DfES, *Higher Standards, Better Schools for All*, white paper (Norwich: TSO, 2005).

And employers also invest considerably in furthering the skills and aptitudes of their own staff, with many businesses now recognising their employees as their principal assets. A survey of employers in 2004 showed that nearly two in three employers (64%) had provided some form of training to staff over the previous 12 months,[46] while recent estimates are that employers invest around £23.5 billion annually in training staff.[47]

Yet despite this progress, expenditure and steadfast commitment, there are signs that young people are still entering organisations without the skills and aptitudes that they need to survive and succeed in modern organisations.

In our GfK NOP survey, 54 per cent of employers agreed that it is becoming harder to find graduate employees with the required workplace skill sets than it was a decade ago, compared

Table 4. *HR directors*: Do you believe it is becoming harder or easier to find potential graduate employees with the required workplace skill sets?

Harder	54%
Easier	16%
No change	26%
Don't know	4%

Source: GfK NOP polling

with just 16 per cent who reported that it is becoming easier (see table 4).

This figure is all the more striking for two reasons:

○ First, there are more graduates than ever entering the job market, as a result of some of the measures discussed earlier in this chapter.
○ Second, employers also reported that graduates in 2006 are *more* skilled than they were a decade ago – 48 per cent agreed with this, compared with 30 per cent who regarded them as less skilled than their counterparts ten years ago.

So what lies behind this story? Why is it that young people are more qualified than ever before, but companies are finding it harder to find the right people?

Does this simply point to a need to raise standards higher still, or is there something else at work?

In the following chapter we argue that we must concern ourselves more with *which* skills and aptitudes we help nurture in young people, rather than simply offering more of the same. While it is clear that higher levels of achievement and vocational learning will remain essential, there is more to preparing young people for adult life.

Education has always been about more than preparing young people for the workplace, but as we begin to value a wider set of characteristics and abilities in the workplace, the *type* as well as the quality of opportunities that we offer young people to learn will become more and more important.

4. Other skills needed

Intelligence is knowing what to do when you don't know what to do.

Jean Piaget

The knowledge economy takes a lot more than knowledge to make it tick. Day-to-day, our use of the word knowledge makes us think about being 'learned' – about being knowledgeable on academic subjects.

But when we think about the jobs that might comprise this new world we think about services like health or even hairdressing, ICT or financial services. Knowledge as we usually think about it is crucial in any one of these areas – there is no doubt that literacy, numeracy and basic ICT skills are necessary skills for success. A hairdresser needs to be able to read the instructions on a chemical hair dye, or enter appointments on a computer. What investment banker is any good without GCSE maths? Vocation-specific knowledge is also clearly vital – the literacy skills that those hairdressers have attained are of no use to customers or to the economy if they do not have the training to do an excellent cut and blow-dry, for example.

But if any one of those professionals fails to engage customers so that they want to make a return visit, present information in such a way that they trust them, or simply smile so they are liked, they are unlikely to generate ongoing business. It takes more than knowledge

Table 5. *HR directors*: What are the top three skills, qualities or aptitudes that you look for in a graduate employee?

Communication/communicating ideas	68%
Problem-solving	40%
Team-working	36%
Creativity and innovation	28%
Ability to work under pressure	26%
Flexibility and multitasking	22%
Customer handling	22%
Numeracy	14%
Literacy	8%

Source: GfK NOP polling

of the 'vocational' skills required, or even excellent literacy and numeracy skills, to be effective in the jobs on offer in the so-called knowledge economy.

This gap between what it takes to be successful and the knowledge we acquire in formal education is often lamented by employers themselves.

Our GfK NOP survey of employers revealed the importance of a set of personal capacities that allow young people to navigate their way around, and succeed within, modern organisations (see table 5).

This is of course a self-selecting group – by definition graduates already have a degree. However, this response from employers points to the importance of a set of aptitudes that make the fruits of a traditional education – whether literacy or a skilled trade – useful inside organisations. Geoff Mulgan, former head of the Prime Minister's Strategy Unit, explains this trend, arguing that, 'turning

Figure 4. Employers' survey: skills in short supply (%)

Technical and practical
Communication
Customer handling
Teamworking
Problem-solving
Literacy
Numeracy
Management
General IT
Office and admin
IT professional
Foreign language

0 5 10 15 20 25 30 35 40 45 50

Source: LSC, *National Employer Skills Survey*, 2004

cognitive skills into career success depends on non-cognitive abilities'.[48] In short, being able to write good essays doesn't necessarily make you good at your job.

A national survey in 2004 of 27,000 employers in total (see figure 4) revealed what is now becoming a familiar pattern.

While the specific location and particular focus of each survey may differ, the evidence is strikingly consistent:

- At the end of last year, a survey for the Edge Foundation found that 67 per cent of employers believed schools were not equipping young people with vital work skills such as team-working, communication and time-keeping.[49]
- In the same survey, 71 per cent said that they would consider hiring young people with poor exam grades who had completed a large amount of work experience.[50]
- A Scottish Enterprise study found that employers judged young people entering their organisations to be most short of oral or communication skills (57%), customer handling (52%), problem-solving (50%) and team-working skills (43%) – compared with written communication (30%), literacy skills (29%) and using numbers (24%).[51]

All the evidence suggests that the capacities that we have often regarded as part of our everyday lives – rather than our careers – are taking on growing importance in the workplace. If innovation flourishes within and across teams, then we need to be able to work within them. If the formalities of hierarchy are being overlaid with social networks inside organisations, then we need to negotiate our way through them.

Yet it seems that graduates are struggling in the face of this challenge. 'Communication' and 'interpersonal skills' are the most often cited of those skills that employers see lacking in new employees leaving education.[52] From our survey of HR directors, 64 per cent said that graduates lack customer handling skills:

Working with people who aren't your age, or who you don't really get on with can be difficult.

All the jobs say 'experience necessary', but where do you get that experience from?

Yet when we asked graduates which situations at work made them feel awkward, their responses were dominated by communication of some description:

○   43 per cent feel awkward challenging senior colleagues
○   35 per cent feel awkward making presentations
○   28 per cent feel awkward speaking in meetings
○   25 per cent feel awkward negotiating
○   one in eight people feel awkward answering the phone.

And this was true across professions – challenging senior colleagues is as awkward in education, manufacturing and production as in the media. Negotiation is as difficult in construction as it is in finance. Qualitative evidence from our focus groups strongly backs this up. Recent graduates commented:

As a trainee solicitor, sharing a room with two paralegals, I was scared of being on the phone, aware that maybe they would be listening to my conversation. It was even worse when I moved into a room with one of the partners!

Being polite is tiring especially in jobs where you face the customer, like in retail.

And if presenting oneself and one's thoughts and opinions is the first challenge, the other side of the communication coin can be even more difficult. Employers in our survey stated that graduates are more than twice as likely to be better at talking and presenting their ideas than they are at listening. There are, perhaps, cultural explanations for this finding: the text message and email generation has relied far less on oral communication than its predecessors, for example.

However, it seems unlikely that the next generation of young people will surrender its laptops in the name of 'communication skills' – and there are some other significant areas in which we might be able to bring about some change. Research for a Creative Partnerships study published this year finds that children in school spend an average of five minutes per day speaking in class.[53] In the education system as it stands, young people are examined to display their knowledge, in written format or sometimes orally. They are not tested for how they listen, respond and adapt to new information.

This starts to unpack why employers regard 'working in a team', 'communication skills' and 'creativity' as such important capacities – and how they relate to each other. If we are poor at communicating with one another, our ability to work together and towards new and productive ideas is fundamentally undermined. Creativity, improvisation and adaptation do not happen in a vacuum; they are either constrained or set free by our ability to relate to one another:

> *It's not like school or university – you can't choose who you work with.*

Employers in our polling rated improvisation second out of 14, in a list of skills that young people tend to be lacking when they enter the workplace – 44 per cent agreed that this is generally the case.

Case study: Improvisation as a business skill

Neil Mullarkey is a comedian and business trainer – he runs courses in improvisation, which he sees as a key skill for succeeding in the world of work.[54] 'When you lose the fear of looking bad, you can look good.' Much of what he helps people to realise is that once you let go of needing to say or do the 'right' thing in a work context, you become free to listen to and build on other people's input. You add value to the conversation. You are not simply looking for the right moment to say what you walked in the room wanting to share and build your reputation on.

For Mullarkey, listening and responding to other people's contributions, with the aim of creating a shared product – just like a jazz group listening to one another and improvising together to co-create a spine-tingling five-bar blues – is a question of effective knowledge management. A constant focus on your own agenda, and not on what you can learn from others too, under-uses the resources at an organisation's disposal.

Being able to listen and respond is not just about the ability to work with peers or managers and build on their skills and ideas. It is also about being able to hear, understand and use criticism constructively, as a positive tool for development. Employers note that the notion of 'appraisal' is one that many young people find difficult. Coming from the 'right or wrong' backdrop of an exams-based education system, ongoing criticism for development can be difficult to use effectively. This is a phenomenon that Paul Black and Dylan Wiliam of King's College would not find surprising. In their seminal text *Inside the Black Box*[55] they argue for a move away from our current 'summative' assessment system that tests what we know at the end of a course or module. Instead, they advocate an assessment system based on formative assessment that uses feedback and criticism as a building block for development. Their assertion is that this makes for more effective learning and learners. As this research shows, it would also make for better employees.

Closely related to this are the demands of risk awareness and risk management. At school we don't do it. Teachers are increasingly risk averse in a litigious world and the strictures of the qualifications pathways that are laid out for young people leave little room for experimentation or deviation. And as Anne Evans, CEO of Heads, Teachers and Industry (HTI), says, this has real consequences for industry.[56] Young people are not equipped to judge independently and adapt to the risks around them in the workplace. The vast majority of workplace accidents involve under-21s and some employers refuse to take on work experience candidates because of the perceived dangers in doing so.

Yet, almost as worrying as the apparent absence of these skills in young people is the fact that many *young people appear not to even realise that they lack them.* In our survey of recent graduates, fully 91 per cent felt that they were either 'quite well' or 'very well' prepared for working life – seemingly contradicting the views of employers that it is becoming harder rather than easier to find the right new recruits (see table 6).

This story is familiar to Tim Bailey, who runs Creative Partnerships

Table 6. *Graduates*: Thinking of the necessary skills needed for a working environment, but not specific on-the-job skills, how well prepared were you with these when embarking on your working career?

Very well prepared	22%
Quite well prepared	69%
Not well prepared	8%
Not at all well prepared	1%

Source: GfK NOP polling

projects in Durham as well as his own architecture firm.[57] In both of these roles he witnesses the difficulties that young people have in 'situating themselves' as he puts it – in 'placing' their ambition and understanding their strengths and weaknesses. He sees this occurring more and more, as the education system unravels young people's independence and imagination, delivering generic skills but unpicking their self-awareness of what they are interested in or need to learn.

Similarly, 'learning to ID yourself' is what Lee Harper-Penman, senior consultant at In-Volve[58] (a charity that works with young people in south London to help them to turn their lives around and get into work) calls this. And it is where all their work with young people starts. Their central programme, RAW, works with young people on the basis that you cannot move forward without understanding who you are and what you really want. You cannot make the most of the opportunities around you without it.

It also starts to explain one of employers' major laments – that even while young people are becoming more skilled, they are less likely to be whole-heartedly committed to a particular sector. It is a quality that the Teach First personnel find only rarely, for example, in the highly trained young people going through its programme, which simultaneously trains graduates to be teachers and business leaders of the future.[59] This is backed up by the testimony of young people themselves:

> *When I finished university, I wasn't very passionate about any career in particular so went to work for a big brand company.*

> *I'm just temping at the moment – I don't really know what I want to do so I'm just doing this to earn some money.*

It seems that young people emerging from the education system at any level – whether the recent graduates in our polling and focus groups, or the young people at In-volve – get a tremendous shock when expected to make independent decisions about their futures. Thirty-four per cent of the employers in our GfK NOP poll felt that self-management is 'the biggest challenge for graduate employees entering employment'. The weight of expectations that are placed on them in advance of going into work, shared milestone after shared milestone, make the task of identifying a personal 'right' first career step, or training opportunity, an extremely difficult one. And one for which young people are unequipped. It is a story that employers and training organisations told us consistently.

This leaves employers with a double dilemma. Not only are graduates under-prepared for what will be required of them, they are also under-prepared for how much there is to learn.

In the next chapter we draw some lessons from projects and partnerships which might point the way to rectifying this.

5. It's not just what you know, it's how you know it

The temptation is to regard the difficulties that young people experience on entering organisations as another set of skills gaps to be plugged – to see 'soft' skills like communication, negotiation and problem-solving as a hole in the toolbox of the economy like the much-publicised dearth of plumbers, or qualified electricians.[60]

Looked at like this, by way of response, new subjects – specifically aimed at addressing these apparent shortfalls – are introduced into mainstream education; citizenship and enterprise education have found their way on to the curriculum, and work experience is now a statutory part of the Key Stage 4 entitlement.

Yet such an approach suffers from a fundamental problem: it equates the acquisition of skills with certain specific subjects, and in doing so fails to penetrate vast swathes of the curriculum. As a result, successive initiatives tend to suffer from making the false – and deeply damaging – distinction between knowledge and skills.

Intuitively we all know that it is impossible to work in a team when there is nothing of substance to work on, but too often the development of a broader set of skills and aptitudes is dismissed as a call for a contentless curriculum, or simply leads to overly mechanical and poorly integrated approaches.

Many schools themselves are already at the vanguard of overcoming this enduring but unhelpful debate; the case study below outlines some of the well-publicised work at Grange Primary School in Derby over the last few years.

Case study: Grange Primary School, Derby[61]

Grange Primary School has made a name for itself in recent years – or rather 'Grangeton', the mini-town set up at the school two years ago by pupils in years 5 and 6.

Grangeton comes alive once a week when 10- and 11-year-olds leave their classes to run the bank, media suite, language café, shop, job centre and a museum that have all been set up there.

Although the school collapses the curriculum to make 'Grangeton' possible, the headteacher insists that *the whole point of Grangeton is to explore the curriculum in new and innovative ways*. The museum – which can be found in a converted storeroom – is a vehicle for discussing the history of the town, while the bank is about maths rather than mortgages. New skills and aptitudes are developed, but only through exploring existing areas of the curriculum.

Personal and social issues are also explored in Grangeton, with young people being asked to explore what they really mean. As the headteacher said recently in an interview with a national newspaper: 'All too often lessons are about theory, "what would you do if?" Here, it is what we will do. Do we sell chocolate bars in the shop, which would up our profits, or do we stick with our principles and offer fruit and healthy alternatives?'

Breaking down the line between knowledge and skills is crucial at every level of schools, colleges or other training organisations to support young people to develop themselves fully, and prevents them from arriving in organisations only to be shocked by the importance of a range of things that they have traditionally regarded as 'extra-curricular'.

Three important characteristics seem to lie at the heart of an approach that has the potential to achieve this systematically, for all young people:

1   the right connections between schools and the wider

community at every level to open up more varied learning opportunities and build understanding

2   an accreditation system that sends the right signals to both professionals and young people and informs about the relative importance these wider skills and aptitudes

3   opportunities that give young people the chance to express themselves and explore their interests.

Connections between the school and the community

As the example of Grange Primary School illustrates, it is entirely possible to provide interesting and creative forms of learning within schools. Schools have been doing so for years. Further, we also know that 'work experience' in the traditional sense can be a dull and distinctly uninformative experience for many young people, who learnt how to make the tea many years before they entered an office:

> *Work experience was a waste of time – I just spent the whole time photocopying.*

However, when genuine partnerships are forged between schools and the wider community they do hold the potential as excellent opportunities for young people to apply their learning, learn more about their own strengths and weaknesses, and tackle problems with a degree of creativity.

The opportunity to tackle a genuine problem in a new environment can offer something new to the experience of schooling. The following case study outlines some of the work being done by an organisation in Scotland called Space Unlimited.

Case study: Space Unlimited, in Scotland[62]

Space Unlimited is about young people solving real-life problems. As an organisation, it sets up projects that give young people the opportunity to address genuine problems facing businesses and other organisations in their local area.

One recent project saw a partnership with Strathclyde Fire & Rescue Service, aimed at trying to address the problem of fire and rescue teams being attacked by young people in their local area. Young people involved in the project were asked to explore the issues, come up with some possible solutions, and to present their findings to the service. Another project saw Space Unlimited working with a healthcare company to try and establish why it is having trouble attracting young people to work there.

One defining feature of a Space Unlimited project is that there is no predetermined answer that young people on each project are working towards, that the teacher knows and they do not, because they are tackling *genuine problems*. This means that things go wrong, and that projects don't always solve the problem that they are asked to tackle. For one well-placed observer, this poses real challenges for professional practice: the instinct is to step in and prevent failure when it seems to be looming for a project, but part of the value of each project is the process of learning the lessons of failure and getting used to facing and overcoming setbacks.

But perhaps the most interesting thing is that each project is very hard to categorise. Is it enterprise education? Or citizenship education? Or work-based learning? Or literacy? Space Unlimited may be funded by Scottish Enterprise, but many of its projects could be described just as easily about citizenship. Each project demands that young people work together to find creative solutions to problems and present their findings, but also that they craft written reports at the end of the process.

As an organisation, Space Unlimited aims to provide 'uniquely valuable experiences that can't be provided in the traditional school setting and which contribute massively to personal development'.[63] Perhaps the most uniquely valuable aspect to it is the way that it avoids one of the core characteristics of many educational projects or packages – it ignores the boundaries between different subjects, between learning and the community, and between 'skills' and 'knowledge'.

The Space Unlimited initiative – and the forms of development that it offers for the young people who get involved – speaks directly to many of the qualities and skills that we have already discussed in this report.

In our GfK NOP survey, companies identified 'problem-solving' as the most important skill for potential graduate employees. Yet it is striking how *unlike* the national curriculum Space Unlimited is, in setting an *open-ended, real-life* problem for *a group* of young people to overcome. The structure of the national curriculum – and, crucially, the way in which young people are examined – is based around pieces of work that are likely to have predetermined answers and which are undertaken in a controlled environment, by individuals working alone with a pen and paper:

> *You're taught the theory, but the practice is totally different.*

Of course, in many schools the effects of this are mitigated against by teaching styles that are able to 'design-in' opportunities for group work, oral contributions and slightly more open-ended projects. But the system as a whole is geared towards what Charles Handy describes as a 'world of certainty'. Reflecting on his own experience of school, he writes:

> *When I went to school, I did not learn anything which I now remember, except this hidden message, that every major problem in life had already been solved. The trouble was that I did not yet know the answers. These answers were in the teacher's head or in her textbook, but not mine. The aim of education, in that world of certainty, was to transfer the answers from the teacher to me, by one means or another. It was a crippling assumption. For years afterwards, when confronted with a problem that was new to me, I ran to an expert. It never occurred to me, in that world of certainty, that some problems were new, or that I might come up with my own answers.*[64]

By giving young people the opportunity to tackle genuine social problems, organisations like Space Unlimited not only help them to apply learning from inside the classroom and explore what concepts like 'citizenship' mean in practice, but they do this is a world where the answers are there to be discovered.

The second important point about the world of *uncertainty* in which the Space Unlimited projects exist is that mistakes are made and things go wrong. This seems like an unlikely starting point for a successful project involving young people – until we recognise that problem-solving itself is an iterative process, in which things often go wrong before they go right.

Whole books have been written on learning from failure, and 'failing forward', but the key point is that this is unlikely to happen if people are so shell-shocked by the effects of an initial setback that they lack the inclination to regroup and revise their approach.

This perhaps explains another important finding from our GfK NOP survey, that when asked which *personal* attributes they look for in potential graduates companies responded with 'resilience', ranking it higher than qualities like 'responsiveness to requests' and 'reliability and punctuality'.

This is not to suggest that all schools need to do is to imitate 'real life', placing banana skins in front of young people in project after project, in order to build their resilience. But it does point to a sense that young people can be profoundly affected by the expectations and experiences that they encounter throughout their education.

If their experiences of learning, and the application and assessment of that learning, take place exclusively in carefully controlled conditions, following a particular pattern, then it should be no surprise that they will develop a certain set of qualities, perhaps at the exclusion of others. Nor should it be surprising that, having overcome all the hurdles and met all the criteria set in front of them during their journey through the education system, young people should emerge blissfully unaware of the importance of a wider set of qualities needed in organisations.

Unquestionably there are ways in which these kinds of opportunities are already being provided across the country *within schools* – through imaginative coursework projects, science experiments, school plays and a whole host of other activities.[65] But the connection with the wider community, under the right circumstances, does provide real potential in helping schools bring together the right ingredients for an enriched experience of learning.

Case study: Heads, Teachers and Industry

Heads, Teachers and Industry maintains that breaking down the divide between knowledge and skills is as much about the experience of teachers, as of students. Truly integrating workplace skills and capabilities into the existing curriculum requires teachers to be imbued with an understanding of what they need to learn to navigate the 'real world' and why. This comprehension needs to be absorbed 'into the DNA of the school' as Anne Evans puts it.[66] And to achieve this requires 'deep immersion'. It is not sufficient to eavesdrop on another world for a few days' work experience and observation. It requires teachers and leaders to become part of the fabric of organisations – taking part in appraisals, training, after-work drinks and anything else that is part of day-to-day working practice.

As Ruth Badger, runner-up in the BBC2's hit series *The Apprentice* says, 'We have a situation in this country where someone who went from school to university to teacher-training college and back to school is teaching children what's required in industry. That's just daft.'[67]

The Teach First programme demonstrates something similar. The newly qualified teachers on this programme are given leadership training from business alongside their classroom experiences to enhance their ability in the classroom as well as open up alternative career paths.[68]

Sending the right signals to young people

An approach that supports schools in providing a greater range of learning opportunities for young people would be an important first step in closing the gap between organisations and young people.

However, the danger is that a more rounded approach is nullified by an examination system which fails to convey the importance of a wider set of skills and aptitudes to either professionals or young people themselves. It is a frequent complaint from the teaching profession that their work is dominated by testing and examinations, but it is important also to consider the messages that our current system of accreditation sends to young people themselves.

In *Living on Thin Air*, Charles Leadbeater describes the difficulties that organisations face in trying to value themselves in a world where their physical assets count for such a small fraction of what they are actually worth. Company brands, the quality of employees, the loyalty of customers are all as important to the total value of companies as the buildings and other physical assets that they tend to own. The assets that we tend to measure, argues Leadbeater, are often far less important than the intangibles that are less easy to quantify.[69] If this applies to companies, could it be true that we face the same problems as individuals? Are we struggling to identify, encourage and accredit the 'intangibles' that make a real difference for young people in organisations?

As Michelle Dewberry, winner of *The Apprentice*, puts it: 'I did think it was important to get qualifications, but only because people are prejudiced against people who don't have them.'[70]

Digby Jones, the outgoing director general of the Confederation of British Industry (CBI), may insist: 'A degree alone is not enough. Employers are looking for more than just technical skills and knowledge of a degree discipline.'[71] But how can we help young people to develop – and demonstrate – these other capacities that are acquiring such importance?

At present this can be seen as a *risk* – a diversion from 'what really counts' – but creative approaches legitimising and accrediting these activities can help. As the following case study shows, there are ways of communicating the importance of wider development to young people.

Case study: Glasgow Caledonian University

Glasgow Caledonian University is following a different model of development from other universities in the city, built around the vice chancellor's aspiration to connect more systematically with the outside world.

To avoid the feeling that anything other than formal study is a diversion, the students' union, working alongside the university itself, has been working to establish an accredited leadership programme for students. The programme is a way for students in existing positions of leadership to develop their skills as young leaders in a series of seminars and workshops. Importantly, though, to take part in and benefit from the programme, students must be in a position of responsibility within the student body – for example, running a society or getting involved in the students' union itself.

On completion of the course, those who have taken part in it receive a letter from the principal to show prospective employers. The programme is designed to benefit all those involved – students with a chance to pursue opportunities for their personal development (and have something to show for it), a university with a more active and participative student body, and employers with a pool of young people more ready for the trials, tribulations and opportunities of the workplace.

Start with people – let young people express themselves

It is one thing to create new opportunities for learning, but it is something else entirely to expect young people to embrace them simply *because they should*.

There are some things that just have to be learnt. We have a national curriculum for a reason. As we highlighted in chapter 2 of this pamphlet, the penalties for not being able to read and write to a high standard are severe later in life. However, some things do not have to be dictated by a national curriculum, or even by adults.

As study after study has shown, young people engage best in developing their own skills and aptitudes when they are given genuinely interesting and exciting opportunities to do so. Starting with people's interests is at the centre of the current drive to tailor services to individuals more effectively, by beginning with individuals rather than rules or institutions. Alan Tuckett, chief executive of NIACE, encapsulates this when he says 'curriculum is motivation'.

Similarly, as previous work done by Demos has shown, the mark of community organisations is that they start with people – building out from their interests to generate and support more active participation:[72]

> *School is very directed. At uni you get much more of a chance to follow your interests.*

This raises some important questions over the suggestion from all three main political parties recently that young people should be required to take part in some form of 'compulsory volunteering' scheme as they make the transition from education and work.

Much like the introduction of enterprise education, this suggestion appears to stem from the diagnosis of a problem – lack of public participation – and lead immediately to an entirely new activity enforced by a degree of compulsion.

However, while the diagnosis may be accurate, the solution, rather like enterprise education, risks seeing participation among young people as a gap to be plugged, rather than an ethos to be embedded in all the opportunities we offer young people in their formative years.

It may be that a volunteering scheme would bring with it some benefits, but it would be a mistake to allow that to obscure the potential that lies in the decade that young people actually spend learning in public institutions.

Further, while volunteering remains an important pursuit, we should not ignore the growing range of activities which many young people are already involved in. Social enterprise is flourishing across the UK, from fair trade coffee to recycling schemes, yet how many young people would turn to their school, university or local council for support in setting up their own enterprise?

So while the government may wish to pursue the idea of a national volunteering scheme, other activities, with other institutional bases, forms of support and personal incentives, need to be recognised:

O   Schools, supported by government could provide financial support for social enterprises led by young people themselves, bringing together funding from citizenship and enterprise education.

O   Schools could work with young people to help access funding made available by the chancellor in the last budget for 'a new a challenge fund – open to all young people proposing innovative projects for youth and community facilities'.[73]

O   As we suggest in the final chapter of this pamphlet, schools and government should find ways of recognising and accrediting these forms of participation.

Each of these steps would help to address the problem rightly identified by politicians from across the political spectrum, but would also help add to the skills set of young people through seeing active participation not just as something to do after several years of learning at school, but as an everyday activity.

An approach to learning, which started from young people's interests – and which involved more than just a spate of enforced volunteering at the end of their educational career – would, therefore, seem an important step in helping to make school more interesting and exciting, and young people more prepared for some of the challenges that lie ahead.

And starting with people and their interests also potentially represents a crucial contribution to the businesses of the future. As we outlined in chapter 2, employers see creativity and innovation as capabilities central to the success of UK plc. Yet, as things stand, graduates display little confidence in their own creativity. In our GfK

NOP survey, recent graduates collectively ranked 'creativity' only eighth out of 12 when asked to identify where their main skills lie – pointing to the importance of finding ways to help young people maintain and develop the creativity that so many children display at an early age before entering formal education.

Anne Evans of HTI sees it as the major ongoing challenge for their organisation to bring into schools.[74] For her, creativity is largely about the attitude it enables – it is about a 'can do' approach to seeing ways around obstacles, rather than stopping in front of them like insurmountable barriers. Creativity is the key tool in developing this attitude – it is what enables us to have the flexibility and adaptability to respond to hurdles as challenges and not as boundaries.

But exercising these skills effectively requires personal motivation – to make the things that we care about happen and to overcome hurdles on the way. Creativity cannot simply be deployed like reading skills. Many young people demonstrate this in their lives beyond school – building websites, making music or even finding ways to sneak out and see their friends when they are meant to be at home. The challenge then is twofold: to find ways of accrediting and valuing these informal examples and of finding ways of better harnessing young people's interests at school.

Chapters 4 and 5 have identified some of the problems that young people are facing on entering organisations. But our research also revealed some of the difficulties that employers themselves are having in attracting, motivating and supporting young people once they arrive in organisations.

So there is one question about equipping young people with the right skills and capacities for the workplace. But there is also another about how employers can fulfil their duty of care towards young people, and make the most of their abilities and interests. We discuss this in the next chapter.

6. It's a two-way street

Thus far, we have discussed the importance of preparing young people for the challenges of future organisations. We have argued that for the disconnect between young people and organisations to be closed we need to offer young people a wider range of opportunities to develop – supported by a wider range of organisations – during their formal education. We need to help young people build a deep understanding of the 'real world' before they get there.

But the challenge of converting young people's intelligence into productive and rewarding work is more than just a question about education, training or even exposure to the world of work. The challenge of understanding is a two-way street – there is a significant gap between employers' offers and graduates' expectations. For organisations, there is an important set of questions about how to attract young people in the first instance – and then motivate, support and help them develop them when they arrive. And there is an increasing business case for doing so.

Of course, the challenge of making organisations happier and more productive places to work has been around for as long as organisations themselves have existed. However, evidence from our opinion polling and elsewhere suggests that this challenge is set to grow in importance against a shifting backdrop of values and social trends.

First among these, as we suggested in chapter 2, are our rising expectations when we enter the market for jobs. Our demands for greater personalisation and improved service as consumers are increasingly matched by our demands for meaning and personal fulfilment in our professional lives:

> *I would prefer working for companies that don't pay as much but treat employees better.*

We already know that graduates are becoming increasingly interested in 'the whole package' offered by employers – a package that allows them to be personally fulfilled inside and outside work, providing purpose and a sense of doing something meaningful in their job, as well as the space to grow and develop outside the workplace:

> *If you enjoy the job, you want to improve the business – this benefits both the company and yourself.*

> *You spend most of your life working, so it's got to be something that gets you out of bed.*

As Dr Nick Baylis, founder of the 'Well-being Institute' at Cambridge University, says in his research into 'young lives':

> *The Zeitgeist for the first decade of the year 2000 promises to be the question: 'How to lead a meaningful and significant life? What is my reason for being?' If the new technologies have been the most dominant feature of the 1990s, individuals have started to reflect upon what on earth they want all that speed-of-light information for in the first place. Because so many of the traditional rule-books and route-maps to life are now outdated or discredited, there is a pervasive fear that our lives will be trivial, and we yearn for some clear cause, some worthy battle that is greater than ourselves.*[75]

Liam Black, head of the Fifteen Foundation, puts it another way. During its recruitment procedures, the foundation does not look for people who want to be involved in the project simply because 'it's better than being on the streets'. It is looking for young people who are fired up by food. Who care about great flavours, quality and new ideas. Without this vehicle and incentive to discover their talent, build true confidence and maintain their commitment, the project would fail.[76]

This fits strongly with what graduates themselves want. In a recent survey[77] 47 per cent of graduates stated that they want to do a job that 'uses their degree'. They want to build their future around an area that means something to them:

If you don't enjoy your job, you are more likely to take it out on the person you are talking to. You get worked up over little things.

We know that there is a business case for this workplace satisfaction in itself. As Richard Freeman of Harvard University illustrates,[78] there is a simple equation that demonstrates clearly that happier workers are less likely to quit, resulting in lower turnover costs for employers. They are more likely to be cooperative and work hard, reducing supervisor costs. And they are also more inclined to accept lower pay – some jobs pay more than others because of the 'disagreeableness of the employments themselves'.[79]

But there is a very particular, longer-term imperative to ensuring that employees personally enjoy and are motivated by what they are doing. The types of skills and capabilities that businesses are increasingly asking young people to deploy demand it.

Zuboff and Maxmin predict that the successful organisations of the future will be those that build services around the complexity of the market and the messiness of people's daily lives.[80] Goods, products or services, they argue, will increasingly revolve around the needs of individuals, with companies pulling together highly personalised packages of support. In this context, the importance of creativity becomes starkly clear. Value is based on our ability to understand and respond to need, regardless of context. It requires that 'can do' attitude, founded on creativity. So whether or not we subscribe to the boundaries of this wholesale 'support revolution', there is no doubt that we will witness a greater personalisation of goods, products and services. The softer skills discussed earlier, along with adaptability and creativity, will be prerequisites for success, regardless of the field a graduate is interested in. And as discussed in chapter 2, our own survey of business leaders confirms the paramount importance of creativity in tomorrow's economy.

So the challenge for employers is similar to that for schools and teachers in the previous chapter. How can we motivate young people to activate and exercise their creativity?

Case study: Ten UK

Alex Cheatle is chief executive of Ten UK. Ten UK is in many ways an exemplar of what organisations and jobs this new economy might hold – it builds services and solutions to meet individuals' needs or problems. They work for customers from pop-stars to head teachers, but in all of those sectors, employees see their job as a 'vocation'. They are committed to and care about finding solutions. 'It wouldn't work otherwise.'

Nick Baylis's research into 'making the most of life' offers a powerful answer. He interviewed hundreds of 'highly accomplished individuals in 1999 and 2000', ranging in age from 16 to 70, about the skills and attitudes that contributed to their success.[81] His findings are grouped according to the themes that emerged strongly – one of which is about stimulating and sustaining motivation:

> *Motivation that comes from inside is the first key ingredient to every successful endeavour. Encourage yourself to find out what thrills you, what suits you, what brings you pride.*
> Baylis interviewee

> *Nobel Laureate, Francis HC Crick, co-discoverer of the formula for DNA, rated his enjoyment of work as the characteristic most*

responsible for his remarkable success, and he placed this ahead of 32 other possible factors.

Baylis interviewee

Alex McLean, a psychologist at Glasgow Education Services, and contributor to the city's Centre for Confidence – a small charity that provides free access to resources to support individuals to build their capacity to deal with the personal and professional challenges of today's world – draws out the implications for the organisations or networks that are in a position to influence that motivation:

The most powerful motivation is self-motivation that comes from within. Motivation is a door that is unlocked from the inside . . . (but) we can have a large role in influencing how others motivate themselves by creating conditions that maximise their assets and help shape how they think about ability, how they approach learning new skills, how they make sense of their progress and how competent they feel.[82]

So there is a role for organisations to support people to motivate themselves. McLean goes on: 'Those who are motivating create a context that maximises the chances of others developing interests.' In other words, in order to activate creativity and adaptability in the employees of tomorrow, organisations need to support young people to better understand and find outlets for their own interests and aspirations.

And this has the potential to contribute to the long-term success of UK plc, as well as its skills requirements in the next five or ten years. Along with a need to be creative in their jobs, we know that graduates are going to have to become extremely flexible and adaptable between jobs:

Our world is changing so rapidly that you can't predict or follow a blueprint of how to conduct your life; you have to be prepared to adapt, and to know how to adapt.

Baylis interviewee

They will need to become extremely effective life-long learners, which requires strong self-awareness of your strengths, weaknesses and the things that inspire you. As one of Baylis's interviewees said:

What have you always enjoyed? Your answer might be a good vantage point from which to see new directions in life.

Baylis interviewee

Ask yourself, 'Do I know what my capabilities are? Where does my potential lie?' That's not to say that's what you'll do, or that's what you'll do for the next ten years, but at least it's a good base to build upon.

Baylis interviewee

Case study: Teach First

Teach First was founded on the basis of research done by McKinsey into how business could better support the community. It places graduates in challenging London and Greater Manchester schools for two years, on the understanding that they will teach for that time, but simultaneously receive training in leadership and other management skills.

The rationale is that the 'soft skills' learned in the classroom are exactly those that employers are looking for. Communication, resilience, innovation and negotiation are all listed in the brochure for potential partner organisations as skills that participants gain. At the same time, the leadership and management training that the young teachers receive helps them to reflect and share 'real world' skills with their pupils:

When you look at Teach First participants, they have a skill set that will be more advanced that others – it's as if they've done a business fundamentals course ahead of joining their employer.

Ian Jordan, Head of Consulting, UK and Ireland, Capgemini

I'll never worry about doing a presentation again.

Teach First participant

This fits strongly with what graduates themselves want. Teach First facilitators stress that the young people who come to them are hungry for a challenge – they want responsibility and the opportunity to 'do' straightaway. They also want and are given the opportunity to retain the flexibility to experiment with their career before committing to an organisation or sector.

In many ways this creates hope for employers if they engage with young people and their existing interests: it holds the promise of a generation of young people more discerning about where they work, but more committed and engaged when they get there.

However, the hope provided by this desire to align work with a wider set of values is tempered by some other findings from our polling and focus groups – that young people frequently feel ill at ease with the formality and structure of organisations.

Employers themselves reported that the biggest challenge for graduate employees was 'fitting into an organisational hierarchy' – a statement agreed with by 40 per cent of respondents, compared with just 10 per cent who agreed the biggest challenge was 'meeting the intellectual challenges of the job'.

And graduates themselves reported that:

O   43 per cent of graduates feel awkward challenging their boss at work – this figure is even higher for women, where it is more than half (53%)
O   only 19 per cent would go to their manager with a problem at work – whereas 50 per cent would go to fellow employees.

In some senses this is a natural reaction to entering a new environment. Particularly at a time when we are unsure of ourselves, we instinctively trust those who are likely to have something in common with us, rather than reverting to senior colleagues whom we are probably trying to impress:

Sometimes you feel like a burden, asking questions all the time.

Case study: The Interns' Network[83]

The Interns' Network was set up in 2003, by a group of (then) interns in response to the dearth of support and information for young people trying to start out in careers in politics and policy. Part of its mission is to give young people a voice in the quality of internships and the equality of access to the opportunities they represent. But a large part of their work is concerned with building connections between young people going through the same experiences. Their fortnightly drinks events allow people to drop in when it suits them to share tips, concerns and perspectives about whether their experience is 'normal' or fair and what they might be able to do about it.

The network is run by interns undergoing the same experiences as its members which keeps the issues and approaches current and relevant. They advertise within organisations and careers services so that young people already know where support might come from in the world of work before they get there. Its membership continues to grow with demand for its services.

However, there is evidence that this tendency to trust others whom we perceive to be like us goes beyond those periods of uncertainty in our lives. Figure 5, from the *Annual Trust Barometer* produced by Edelman,[84] demonstrates a tendency for us to trust peers, or 'people like me' even ahead of doctors, academics and representatives of non-governmental organisations.

These figures point to the decline in deference to formal positions and institutions, and reflect the growing number of opportunities that people have to draw on each other's opinions now. In particular, these opportunities have exploded through the possibilities opened up by the internet: we now decide whether to enter into deals with sellers on eBay through studying feedback provided by their peers; we buy books on amazon.com if other readers have rated them highly;

Figure 5. Credibility of spokespeople

When forming an opinion of a company, how credible would the information be from ...

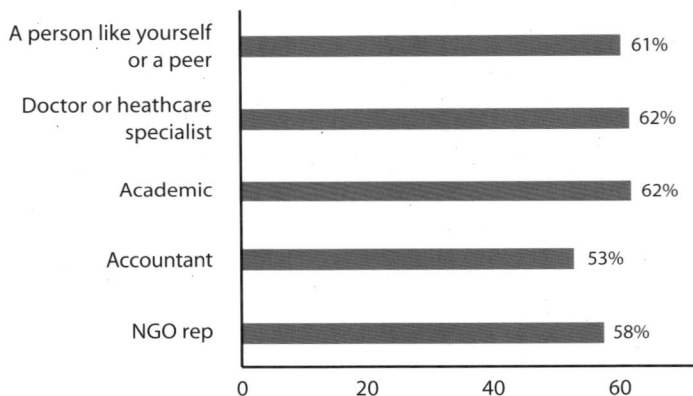

A person like yourself or a peer	61%
Doctor or heathcare specialist	62%
Academic	62%
Accountant	53%
NGO rep	58%

Includes interviews conducted in the UK, France, Germany, Italy and Spain
Source: Edelman, *2006 Annual Trust Barometer*

and we interact with countless numbers of peers through blogging, discussion threads and chat rooms.

And the evidence is that this extends beyond the internet – a survey undertaken for World Book Day in 2005 revealed that 'word of mouth' ranked above the title, appearance, synopsis or even advertising for a book as a factor in influencing whether people decided to read it or not.[85]

In a world where peer-to-peer interaction is more possible, more pervasive – and more useful – than ever before, it is perhaps unsurprising that young people turn to their peers rather than their superiors for advice and support.

Case study: Future Foundations

Future Foundations is a coaching and mentoring organisation that has been developed for young people, by young people. Its website states: 'Having experienced firsthand the problems that stem from the severe lack of guidance and encouragement for university leavers, our founders spent 18 months researching graduate challenges, and finding the solutions that fix them.'[86]

The organisation's courses and coaching mix personal development with 'soft skills training for the real world and your career'. The skills they identify are aligned closely with those that employers say they want to see: 'The Future Foundations course teaches people how to master their emotions, build confidence, present in public effectively, sell themselves and their ideas, make a report, deal with people, set goals, understand time and money and enhance your leadership skills.'

Interestingly, this peer-led organisation represents one of the few examples of work experience aimed at responding to young people's lack of clarity about what 'career' to pick. And their unwillingness to commit 'too soon':

'Sparkle rotation' is a scheme which allows graduates three months' experience in each of several industries. This is great for graduates who are not sure which career path to take and would like to base their decisions on firsthand knowledge of the working world.

This combination of factors – uncertainty in new environments, and a culture increasingly built around peer-to-peer interaction – has some potentially important implications for companies. In our focus groups graduates stressed that one of the key attractions of graduate schemes was not just the career opportunities, but the knowledge that others 'like me' would be starting work at the same time – and that there would be people a year further on with tips and hints to share. In this sense, graduate schemes seem to be regarded by many not just as a step on the ladder up in organisations, but also as an invaluable support network.

This may be important for companies as they seek to attract the best graduates, but also provides some hints about how they might be supported once they are inside organisations. It suggests that young people tend to benefit from a 'one up, one across' support structure – where they have people to go to for advice and guidance who are either a year on from them, or who are likely to be experiencing similar problems to them at present.

This points to the value of mentoring schemes for young people, with people that they can relate to, but also to management practices that help to nurture the social networks that young people value as safety nets when they arrive in organisations. It may be, for example, that rather than simply surrounding young employees with senior staff in their first weeks and months at work, also take care to ensure that new employees have sufficient opportunities to work with and meet each other in those early days. This may be within or beyond the organisation, with other young people going through similar experiences.

> **Case study: Mentoring and peer support at the School for Social Entrepreneurs**
>
> The School for Social Entrepreneurs (SSE) in Bethnal Green – which takes university graduates alongside those who left school at 18 – has built much of its training around mentoring and peer support.
>
> All students have their own mentor – in this case someone from outside the organisation – and the school uses 'action learning sets' as a way of helping entrepreneurs support each other's projects.
>
> Action learning sets are small groups meeting to talk intensively about the difficulties people are encountering in their projects. People can ask each other questions, but do not give advice. Nick Temple, who works at the SSE, argues that this form of peer

support can be invaluable, giving students the chance to be open and honest and to learn from each others' experiences.

But professional development is not the only arena in which young people want employers to be more attuned to their needs. The other part of the 'whole package' that young people are craving is for work–life balance:

> Employers expect you to sacrifice your life, for example one friend was made to expect and respond to an email in the middle of the night. Most people want a decent life.

This emphasis on the overall quality of people's experiences at work – which includes, but is not restricted to, the level of remuneration that they receive – helps explain the growing importance of work–life balance as an issue for people entering organisations.

In our GfK NOP survey, four in ten graduates identified this as a problem, saying that they found it 'difficult' to maintain a balance (see table 7).

As might be expected, our focus groups revealed antipathy towards employers unwilling to recognise this as an issue. And in some senses this plays into the never-ending debate that we describe in the introduction to this pamphlet – where employers voice anger at

Table 7. Graduates: How easy do you find it to keep a balance between your work and home life?

Very easy	13%
Easy	50%
Hard	33%
Very hard	4%
Source: GfK NOP polling	

graduates' shortcomings, while graduates themselves feel down-trodden and disappointed by their quality of life after graduation:

It's all work, work, work . . . I want to move to Australia – there's a greater focus on quality of life there.

There just aren't enough hours between 9 and 5.

Companies try and squeeze out as much as they can as they are there to make money.

However, both our focus groups and opinion polling also revealed a sense that work–life balance represents more than a company policy – that it can also be understood as a *skills set*. When asked, a third of graduates reported that they lacked work–life balance skills when they first entered organisations after university:

Learning to live well is a skill, just like swimming. And like swimming, it can go from being about sheer survival, to being highly pleasurable, all depending on your level of competence.
Baylis interviewee

While this may also not be surprising – being a student brings with it many challenges, but work–life balance is not generally regarded as one of them – it does represent an opportunity for employers to work alongside young people to help them to survive and succeed in organisations. Work–life balance skills might mean anything from successful time management to training on how to make best use of mobile technology.

As recent research by the Henley Centre has shown, technology is neither empowering nor imposing in and of itself – the key point is 'the way in which people use it'.[87] Our own survey demonstrated this point, with 43 per cent of graduates reporting that technology has made it 'easier' to maintain work–life balance, compared with 19 per cent who felt it had made maintaining a balance harder.

On this basis, there is an opportunity for those companies that genuinely take work–life balance seriously to help equip young people with the skills they need to translate a company policy into an everyday reality. This might mean employers including work–life balance training as part of their initial induction for new employees, and then including it as one element of people's overall performance in appraisals. Could you be denied promotion one day for working too hard?

Case study: In Equilibrium, in-house 'lifestyle management' courses[88]

In Equilibrium's clients include Amnesty International, BAE Systems, Ikea, UNISON, University of Westminster, E2V Technologies and Inland Revenue, representing the cross-sectoral relevance of their work.

They offer a variety of services including a one-day interactive training course for individuals. This aims 'to equip participants with the knowledge, tools and techniques that will reduce their stress and boost their health and wellbeing'. The objectives of these sessions include:

O   effective and proven switching-off skills they can use to relax, recover and get a good night's sleep
O   an understanding of how small lifestyle changes can make a big difference
O   how to use powerful cognitive techniques to change their perspective on life and work.

Previous participants have reported a better understanding of how their lifestyle affects their health and their vulnerability to stress, an increased awareness of what causes their stress and enhanced ability to relax and switch off as soon as they get home.

The aim of this would not be to transfer responsibility for work–life balance entirely away from employers to young people, but to recognise that employers can help employees to help themselves if they are really serious about work–life balance – and also to open up spaces for conversations between employees and employers on the subject.

Support

Some employers are going further than helping people to address work–life balance issues – they are helping to address people's 'life' issues through work. The following case study of ARUP, the business consultants, explores how some companies are beginning to collapse the distinction between 'work' and 'life' in the support they offer to their employees.

Case study: Solving 'life' issues through work at ARUP

ARUP are business consultants. They have over 7000 staff working in 70 offices in more than 30 countries. And they provide tailored support to those staff through a benefits package in partnership with a company named Employee Assistance Resource (EAR).

People at ARUP are entitled to the advice and support because they are employees, but the advice that they request and receive could be on a whole host of issues. EAR is there to help you if you find your children using drugs, if your partner asks you for a divorce, or if an unwelcome, unwieldy or unexpectedly large bill arrives in the post.

The support that EAR offers turns the story of work–life balance on its head. No longer is it a story of keeping 'work' and 'life' artificially parcelled off from one another: it recognises that work and life are inevitably entwined and that 'life' issues can be solved, rather than ignored, at work.

This might be understood as moving beyond a deficit model of work–life balance. The approach of ARUP – perhaps a working example of what has been termed 'deep support' – is less about walling off 'home' and 'life' from each other, and more about recognising that the two will always be interlinked to some degree:

You take your work home, but also your home issues to work.

There is good reason to suggest that this applies to young graduates more than ever before; a recurrent theme in our focus groups was the challenge of sudden financial independence for many, coupled with rising levels of student debt, and – for many graduates – the need to adjust to a new start in a new city. So, if we worry about problems in our home life when we're at work, why not solve them there?

> *Moving to London wasn't such a big thing for me – coming from the North I'd been away for uni and things, so it was just another move. But for some people, that's really hard.*

> *I've aged ten years in three months!*

It is these pressures that have led Future Foundations to add an optional extra to their graduate course:

> *Gradworld . . . what you need to know about life as a graduate covers all the practical aspects of graduate life – paying tax, handling paying back student loans, dealing with landlords, tenancy agreements, pension plans, insurance cover, graduate banking, and setting up as self-employed.*[89]

The origins of the word health offer a strong case for the ongoing importance of this kind of support. The word 'health' literally means 'wholeness', and the verb 'to heal' literally means 'to make whole'. We are all whole people, so where we are unsettled or experiencing problems in one area of our lives, it is inevitable that it will impact on the rest. So investing in our personal wellbeing clearly has professional benefits.

This chapter has looked at the disconnect between young people from the other side of the usual debates – how employers are often failing to understand the needs of young people – and the mutual benefits that could be derived from bridging this gap.

The final chapter offers some recommendations that look at how 'reconnection' might be achieved from both sides.

7. Reconnection

Previous chapters have thrown into stark relief a number of disconnects in different dimensions. Employers want one set of things and graduates deliver another. Graduates demand more and different things from their lives, and employers have not yet figured out how to respond. Employers want more training for young people but the money going in is not making a transformative impact.

But looking at these disconnects in depth – understanding the qualities that employers are after and the quality of life that young people want to achieve – illustrates that the system as it stands represents faulty or loose connections more than any fundamental incompatibility. It becomes clear that the components of this system could and should match up.

Employers want more versatile, responsive and personable employees able to deploy different facets of their personality effectively in a given situation. Young people want to lead rich, challenging lives with a healthy balance between home and the workplace and jobs that reflect their values and their interests. There is undoubted overlap. And rewiring the connections between them potentially represents the added value that young people, employers and politicians are all looking for.

Looked at like this, it is unsurprising that current government investment in young people and skills is not making the kind of impact that employers want to see – and subsequently, is not fuelling the acceleration in productivity that is required for UK plc to catch up with its competitors. Putting more money in the same places will not change the communication and interrelationships between young people, businesses and the education system.

Reconnection has to happen at every level. It is not enough simply to equip young people with another set of skills as they exit the education system at whatever level. As our research shows there is a hidden organisational curriculum already embedded in schools, colleges and universities. Young people enter the world of work thinking they are prepared – but prepared for a different world of individual study, tightly defined problems and questions and success measured on displaying one's knowledge.

Equally, it is not enough for people to learn to be flexible, creative, innovative and resilient at school or college if employers cannot respond to the people they have recruited and create the environments in which they will best be able to deploy these capabilities in organisations.

Reconnection is a long-term strategy for success. One of the strongest messages from both employers and graduates is one of uncertainty. Organisations are here to stay, but the form they will take is unclear – there is evidence of both 'hyperorganisation' and 'disorganisation'. Employers know that the skills they require from young people are changing, but are unsure of exactly what they will want from them in the future. The need for creativity and adaptability in the employees of the future are the only definite prerequisites. Young people themselves know they want their working lives to reflect their personal values, but are unclear how to achieve this. And they are all different. There is no silver bullet answer for employers to respond to whole cohorts of people.

In this world, the ability of organisations and employees to respond and adapt will be the pillars of success, so constant dialogue and ongoing efforts at mutual understanding and support will be key. Reconnection does not just enable young people to be better prepared for the demands of today's workplace. It potentially supports young people to shape the workplaces of tomorrow to meet their changing aspirations and employers to help education and training respond to the inevitable and as yet unseen challenges of the future.

Recommendation 1

The Government should introduce a Skills Portfolio, to help capture some of the learning, skills and aptitudes that are often not reflected in traditional qualifications. This portfolio should include the following characteristics:

○ It would aim to bring together some of the skills/capacities that are presently hinted at, but not accredited in, Citizenship Education and Enterprise Education – alongside the skills that the best teaching already produces across the curriculum. Young people today would need to demonstrate the ability to work in a team, to come up with and act on new ideas, to demonstrate presentation skills, and to take part in some kind of overall reflection on the task. The exact content would be flexible over time to reflect the changing demands of the workplace. This reflection, or self-evaluation, would be demonstrated through some kind of artefact which could be anything from a written report to a short film.

○ It would be jointly awarded by schools *and an external partner*. This would help to encourage schools to forge partnerships with other organisations and groups within the wider community. The partnering organisation could be a charity – for example the Prince's Trust – or a business willing to participate in the scheme.

○ The portfolio would not be compulsory. Schools (and pupils and parents) would be free to make decisions about whether young people attempted to gain the Skills Portfolio. The aim of this would be to ensure that the qualification was genuinely demand-led – if businesses were willing to take a leadership role and support the development and accreditation of some of the skills they say young people need, then the qualification would be likely to enjoy high take-up rates. Should businesses not take a lead – and fail to emphasise the portfolio in recruitment decisions – then the portfolio would simply wither away. This implies a leadership role for large businesses, but also for organisations like the CBI and the British Chambers of Commerce in supporting new approaches to learning.

O   The portfolio would be won through involvement in a practical project, but that project could – and ideally would – form part of the existing curriculum or existing informal activities that young people do outside school. For example, it may come through a practical piece of coursework, or through a citizenship or enterprise project involving an external partner.

O   Young people should be given as much ownership as possible over the activities that they took part in to gain the portfolio. Where possible, projects should start from their interests and work back to areas of the curriculum as they are designed in more detail.

Recommendation 2

Schools should hold termly equivalents of 'parents' evenings' for local businesses and community organisations. The aim of this would be to help support a greater degree of dialogue between schools and the wider community, helping to support a wider range of partnerships and a greater degree of mutual understanding.

Schools already invest time in holding conversations because they recognise their importance in educating young people successfully. The same process of dialogue should take place between schools and the wider community.

Recommendation 3

The government should support the introduction of an Investors in Community accreditation for businesses. This accreditation would be similar to the Investors in People badge, which already exists. The aim of this would be to encourage a greater number of partnerships between the education system and wider community, through providing clearer information to prospective employees and customers about companies' contributions to their local areas.

The timing is right for this step: consumer and employer values are shifting, all the main political parties have renewed their interest in building strong communities, and much of the thinking around an accreditation of this sort is already being done by a coalition of organisations pulled together by Business in the Community (BiTC).

To mark the twentieth anniversary of BiTC's PerCent club – a voluntary benchmark measuring the contributions made by companies though cash donations, staff time, gifts in kind and management time to the wider community – the review is seeking to create a standard of excellence to which businesses will aspire and that customers will recognise. This could well provide the basis for a renowned national accreditation to match that of Investors in People.

Recommendation 4

Universities should draw on the work being done at universities like Glasgow Caledonian University and MIT-Cambridge to embed transferable, work-based skills into the curriculum. This would see undergraduates applying their skills in at least two or three real-life settings before receiving their degree, as an integral part of the curriculum. The benefits of this would be manifold. First, it would of course help to build the transferable and 'softer' skills that employers want from graduate employees, before entering the workplace permanently. Second, it would build undergraduates' capacity and belief in their adaptability to different settings, before they have to risk it alone. Third, it would help to refine graduates' ideas for the areas in which they might like to work. Finally, by including this element in all university courses, it would start to break down the perceived and damaging status gap between academic and vocational skills. By explicitly attributing value to real-life skills in already respected settings, the common importance of vocational aptitudes across subjects would be given real currency.

Recommendation 5

Companies should hold entrance interviews and skills audits for young people entering their organisations. The advantage of this would go beyond finding out what young people's development needs are. It would help managers to understand what drives and motivates their new recruits, as well as sending the message that it matters. Furthermore, it would also encourage young people entering organisations to think more explicitly about their strengths and weaknesses, giving them a stronger platform on which to build their professional identity, their own investment in their development and any future career moves.

Recommendation 6

Companies should recognise work–life balance as a set of skills as well as a set of legal obligations or company policy. To this end, all young people entering organisations should be given some work–life balance training as a matter of course, like that offered by In Equilibrium. Training for new technology should include guidance not just about how to work with new technology, but also how to fit that technology into people's lives. Employers might see this as the natural extension of existing non-pecuniary benefits. Many already offer free gym membership or private health insurance. Training for better psychological health is the natural complement, as well as being the key to unlocking the value of everything else on offer – what good is gym membership if you are too exhausted or time-poor to enjoy it? Employees' work–life balance should be monitored alongside their performance in other areas of work.

The aim of this is not to replace company policies but to make sure that those policies are translated into everyday realities. Recognising work–life balance as a skill and including it in performance appraisals would be aimed at starting more conversations between organisations and employees about work–life balance and how they could work to improve it in a mutually beneficial way.

Recommendation 7

Companies should learn from leading practice and provide 'deep support' for young people entering organisations. Rather than simply aiming to 'wall off' home and work, many organisations are beginning to help solve people's 'life' issues at work, through offering services from legal advice to dry cleaning. With organisations competing for talent on values and ethos as well as pay, this would help demonstrate a positive attitude towards employees. It would also reflect the fact that graduates face a range of issues and challenges on leaving university – including managing debt, finding accommodation, entering full-time employment for the first time for many and maintaining personal relationships – in entirely new settings.

Recommendation 8

Employers should work with each other, and with young people, to develop an online, open-access training resource that young people can consult when they need to, to supplement their own development. One part of the website would be used to display resources that collaborating employers have all agreed are of value, which contribute to personal development and are important to some or all contributors. This might be workplace based or related to the work–life balance or 'deep support' issues discussed above. The other part would be dedicated to open and collaborative development of new resources – things that young people or employers perceive a demand for. A governing board, representative of contributing employers and their new employees, would form the quality assurance panel that would allow resources to be moved from the development side to the display side of the site. This would be similar in structure to the Open University's proposed open educational resource.[90]

This would link crucially with young people's increased self-awareness of their own skills needs from the audits at the beginning of their time in a new organisation. It would be a tool for helping to grow young people's (and employers') awareness of their development needs as well as fulfilling existing training requirements – other resources on offer could act as suggestions for growth opportunities. Finally, with dynamic, ongoing development, this resource would avoid becoming 'out of date'.

Recommendation 9

Organisations should find ways to support the peer-to-peer networks, both inside and outside their walls, that young people rely on and value so highly when they enter organisations. This might include arranging mentoring relationships with employees who were in their position not long ago, and trying to ensure that new employees are not surrounded just by senior colleagues when they first enter organisations. The opportunity to share experiences and puzzle through common problems is an important addition to the more formal procedures set in place within organisations.

It would also include recognising and promoting trusted 'partner' peer organisations of young people offering mutual, independent support during similar experiences. Again, these might be work-based, like Future Foundations or the Interns' Network, or related to the deep support discussed earlier.

Recommendation 10

Companies should consider organising themselves into networks, offering short-term 'skills development' contracts for new graduates, involving placements in a number of different companies or institutions. Ideally, these networks would involve public, private and voluntary sector employers looking to develop young talent. These would not simply be internships. They would be paid positions, with real responsibility and meaningful roles, all of which share similar skills in different contexts.

By providing a rich and exciting range of experiences to potential new employees, organisations would benefit from attracting a more diverse and interesting range of young people. Further, by removing the apprehension of taking a 'permanent' first step into the workplace, employers may also be more successful in attracting the more 'promiscuous' but talented graduates who are unsure about committing to a career path at 21. As the experience of Teach First shows, many of these graduates never leave the career that that they join on a 'temporary' basis, but the prospect of not feeling locked into a permanent contract is a liberating one.

Finally, employers and employees would both benefit from the chance for graduates to experience different workplaces, work cultures, conventions and challenges. Young people would not only pick up new skills through exposure to a range of different situations, but this would help them gain greater *awareness* of their own capabilities and development needs for the future.

A perfect world of multiskilled, highly socialised young people entering organisations that are aligned with their human values, supportive of work–life balance and offer a helping hand to solve life issues are not going to be developed overnight. Everyone may not be able to win all of the time. But by taking a range of practical steps there are ways in which we can begin to move beyond the stasis of the current debate.

Through re-thinking how we prepare people for organisations, and then helping them to identify and build on their talents within them, we can start to reconnect young people and organisations – and move closer to realising the twin aspirations of productive and happy workplaces.

Notes

1   Business in the Community, *FastForward Research* (London: BITC/NOP, 2002).
2   K Robinson, *Out of Our Minds: Learning to be creative* (Oxford: Capstone Publishing, 2001).
3   T Bentley, *Learning Beyond the Classroom: Education for a changing world* (London: Routledge/Demos, 1998).
4   G Brown, speech to the Trades Union Congress, 13 Sept 2005.
5   For example, as Chris Humphries illustrates in *Skills in a Global Economy* (London: City & Guilds, 2005), some occupations will suffer considerably less than others from the effects of an ageing population.
6   P Brown and H Lauder, *Capitalism and Social Progress: The future of society in a global economy* (Basingstoke: Palgrave, 2001).
7   J Wilsdon and C Leadbeater, *The Atlas of Ideas* (London: Demos, forthcoming).
8   HM Treasury, *Productivity in the UK: The evidence and the government's approach* (London: HM Treasury, 2004).
9   C Handy, *Beyond Certainty: The changing worlds of organisations* (London: Hutchinson, 1995).
10   F Levy and RJ Murname, *The New Division of Labor: How computers are creating the next job market* (Princeton, NJ: Princeton University Press, 2004).
11   G Brown, speech to the Smith Institute, 'Globalisation and progressive politics' event, London, 28 Mar 2006.
12   G Cox, *Cox Review of Creativity in Business: Building on the UK's strengths* (London: HM Treasury, 2005).
13   R Florida, *The Rise of the Creative Class* (New York: Basic Books, 2002).
14   T Bentley, *Learning Beyond the Classroom.*
15   T Smit, *Eden* (London: Bantam Books, 2001).
16   H Lownsbrough, G Thomas and S Gillinson, *Survival Skills: Using life skills to tackle social exclusion* (London: Demos, 2004).
17   P Skidmore, 'Leading between', in H McCarthy, P Miller and P Skidmore (eds), *Network Logic: Who governs in an interconnected world?* (London: Demos, 2004).

18   P Miller and P Skidmore, *Disorganisation: Why future organisations must 'loosen up'* (London: Demos, 2004).
19   MORI poll, *Innovation Survey*, carried out on behalf of CBI and QinetiQ (London: MORI, 2005).
20   HM Treasury, 'Advancing enterprise: enterprise in global markets', conference, London, 4 Feb 2005.
21   G Brown, speech to the TUC.
22   'Creative types give companies an edge', *The Times*, 26 Jan 2006.
23   R Semler, *Maverick: The success story behind the world's most unusual workplace* (London: Random House Business Books, 2001).
24   JP Andrew, *Innovation 2005: Senior management survey*, Boston Consulting Group, see www.bcg.com/publications/publications_search_results.jsp?PUBID=1312 (accessed 16 May 2006).
25   Miller and Skidmore, *Disorganisation*.
26   Common Purpose, *Searching for Something: Exploring the career traps and ambitions of young people* (London: Common Purpose, 2004).
27   Presentation by Ben Page, 'Understanding trust in a "show me" world', MORI/Demos seminar, Apr 2006.
28   Business in the Community, *FastForward Research*.
29   'When social issues become strategic', *McKinsey Quarterly*, Apr 2006.
30   S Zuboff and J Maxmin, *The Support Economy: Why corporations are failing individuals and the next episode of capitalism* (New York: Viking, 2004).
31   D Coats, *Agenda for Work* (London: Work Foundation, 2005).
32   Miller and Skidmore, *Disorganisation*.
33   'Collective failure', *Guardian*, 22 Apr 2006.
34   City & Guilds, *Portfolio Careers* (London: City & Guilds, 2004).
35   Miller and Skidmore, *Disorganisation*.
36   Report of the Orange Future Enterprise Commission, *Organisational Lives: Inventing the future with mobile technology* (Henley: Henley Centre, Headlight Vision, 2006).
37   Robinson, *Out of Our Minds*.
38   F Hirsch, *The Social Limits to Growth* (London: Routledge, 1977), Quoted in P Brown, A Hesketh and S Williams, *The Mismanagement of Talent: Employability and jobs in the knowledge economy* (New York: Oxford University Press, 2004).
39   Department for Education and Skills, *Skills: Getting on in business, getting on at work, Part 1*, white paper (Norwich: TSO, 2005).
40   Leitch Review of Skills, *Skills in the UK: The long-term challenge*, interim report (London: HM Treasury, 2005).
41   Ibid.
42   Ibid.
43   Humphries, *Skills in a Global Economy*.
44   Leitch Review of Skills, *Skills in the UK*.
45   KPMG, 'Competitive alternatives report', 2002.
46   Learning and Skills Council, *National Employer Skills Survey* (London: LSC, 2004).

47   Leitch Review of Skills, *Skills in the UK.*
48   G Mulgan, *Learning to Serve: The toughest skills challenge for public services and government and what can be done about it* (London: Learning and Skills Development Agency, 2006).
49   'School "doesn't prepare pupils for work"', *Education Guardian*, 19 Dec 2005, see http://education.guardian.co.uk/schools/story/0,5500,1670853,00.html (accessed 19 May 2006).
50   Ibid.
51   Hall Aitken, *Demand for Skills and Training in the Scottish Borders: The employers' view* (Galashiels: Scottish Enterprise Borders, 2003).
52   LSC, *National Employer Skills Survey.*
53   S Brice Heath, E Paul-Boehnck and S Wolf, *Made for Each Other* (forthcoming).
54   Interview with Neil Mullarkey, 1 Mar 2006.
55   P Black and D Wiliam, *Inside the Black Box: Raising standards through classroom assessment* (London: Kings College, 1998).
56   Interview with Anne Evans, 12 Jan 2006.
57   Interview with Tim Bailey, 16 Jan 2006.
58   See www.in-volve.org.uk/Involve/index.aspx (accessed 16 May 2006).
59   Interview with Brett Wigdortz, CEO, Teach First, 18 Apr 2006.
60   LSC, *National Employer Skills Survey.*
61   This case study is drawn from 'Where pupils run the town', *Times Education Supplement*, 22 Oct 2004, and 'Look back in wonder', *Guardian*, 13 Jul 2004.
62   See www.spaceunlimited.org/ (accessed 19 May 2006).
63   Interview with Heather Sim, Space Unlimited, 15 Dec 2005.
64   C Handy, *Beyond Certainty: The changing worlds of organisations* (London: Hutchinson, 1995).
65   In 2005 a report from the National Endowment for Science, Technology and the Arts (NESTA) highlighted the importance of the 'intellectual discipline of science and the excitement of exploring the unknown', in scientific experiments in the classroom. See *Real Science: Encouraging experimentation and investigation in school science learning* (London: NESTA, 2005).
66   Interview with Anne Evans.
67   V Lee and D Smith, 'Meet the Wendys: Britain's brightest entrepreneurs', *Observer*, 7 May 2006, see http://observer.guardian.co.uk/uk_news/story/0,,1769394,00.html (accessed 22 May 2006).
68   Interview with Brett Wigdortz.
69   C Leadbeater, *Living on Thin Air: A blueprint for the new economy* (London: Penguin, 2000).
70   Lee and Smith, 'Meet the Wendys'.
71   D Jones, Director-General, Confederation of British Industry, Foreword to *Prospect Directory* 2004/5, see www.prospects.ac.uk/cms/ShowPage/Home_page/What_do_graduates_do__20 06/Employability_and_myths_uncovered/p!epmigXc (accessed 16 May 2006).
72   J Craig and P Skidmore, *Start With People: How community organisations put citizens in the driving seat* (London: Demos, 2005).

73   G Brown, Chancellor of the Exchequer's budget statement, 22 Mar 2006.

74   Interview with Anne Evans.

75   N Baylis, 'A bird's eye view of the research findings', see www.younglivesuk.com (accessed 19 May 2006).

76   Interview with Liam Black, 18 Jan 2006.

77   Teach First brochure for graduates, 2006, see www.teachfirst.org.uk/ (accessed 18 May 2006).

78   R Freeman, 'Love your job or hate it? The economics of job satisfaction', public lecture, Centre for Economic Performance, LSE , 8 May 2006.

79   A Smith, *An Inquiry into the Nature and Causes of the Wealth of Nations*, ed Edwin Cannan (London: Methuen and Co., Ltd, 1904, 5th edn; first published 1776).

80   Zuboff and Maxmin, *The Support Economy*.

81   See www.younglivesuk.com/ (accessed 19 May 2006).

82   See www.centreforconfidence.co.uk/pp/index.php?p=c2lkPTEx (accessed 19 May 2006).

83   See www.internsnetwork.org.uk (accessed 22 May 2006).

84   Edelman, *2006 Annual Trust Barometer*, see www.edelman.com (accessed 22 May 2006).

85   'Word of mouth "winner for books"', *BBC Online*, 3 Mar 2005.

86   See www.future-foundations.co.uk/ (accessed 22 May 2006).

87   Orange Future Enterprise Commission, *Organisational Lives*.

88   See www.in-equilibrium.co.uk/ (accessed 16 May 2006).

89   See www.future-foundations.co.uk/ (accessed 16 May 2006).

90   See http://oci.open.ac.uk/pressrelease.html (accessed 16 May 2006).

Copyright

DEMOS – Licence to Publish

THE WORK (AS DEFINED BELOW) IS PROVIDED UNDER THE TERMS OF THIS LICENCE ("LICENCE"). THE WORK IS PROTECTED BY COPYRIGHT AND/OR OTHER APPLICABLE LAW. ANY USE OF THE WORK OTHER THAN AS AUTHORIZED UNDER THIS LICENCE IS PROHIBITED. BY EXERCISING ANY RIGHTS TO THE WORK PROVIDED HERE, YOU ACCEPT AND AGREE TO BE BOUND BY THE TERMS OF THIS LICENCE. DEMOS GRANTS YOU THE RIGHTS CONTAINED HERE IN CONSIDERATION OF YOUR ACCEPTANCE OF SUCH TERMS AND CONDITIONS.

1. **Definitions**
   a **"Collective Work"** means a work, such as a periodical issue, anthology or encyclopedia, in which the Work in its entirety in unmodified form, along with a number of other contributions, constituting separate and independent works in themselves, are assembled into a collective whole. A work that constitutes a Collective Work will not be considered a Derivative Work (as defined below) for the purposes of this Licence.
   b **"Derivative Work"** means a work based upon the Work or upon the Work and other pre-existing works, such as a musical arrangement, dramatization, fictionalization, motion picture version, sound recording, art reproduction, abridgment, condensation, or any other form in which the Work may be recast, transformed, or adapted, except that a work that constitutes a Collective Work or a translation from English into another language will not be considered a Derivative Work for the purpose of this Licence.
   c **"Licensor"** means the individual or entity that offers the Work under the terms of this Licence.
   d **"Original Author"** means the individual or entity who created the Work.
   e **"Work"** means the copyrightable work of authorship offered under the terms of this Licence.
   f **"You"** means an individual or entity exercising rights under this Licence who has not previously violated the terms of this Licence with respect to the Work, or who has received express permission from DEMOS to exercise rights under this Licence despite a previous violation.
2. **Fair Use Rights.** Nothing in this licence is intended to reduce, limit, or restrict any rights arising from fair use, first sale or other limitations on the exclusive rights of the copyright owner under copyright law or other applicable laws.
3. **Licence Grant.** Subject to the terms and conditions of this Licence, Licensor hereby grants You a worldwide, royalty-free, non-exclusive, perpetual (for the duration of the applicable copyright) licence to exercise the rights in the Work as stated below:
   a to reproduce the Work, to incorporate the Work into one or more Collective Works, and to reproduce the Work as incorporated in the Collective Works;
   b to distribute copies or phonorecords of, display publicly, perform publicly, and perform publicly by means of a digital audio transmission the Work including as incorporated in Collective Works;
   The above rights may be exercised in all media and formats whether now known or hereafter devised. The above rights include the right to make such modifications as are technically necessary to exercise the rights in other media and formats. All rights not expressly granted by Licensor are hereby reserved.
4. **Restrictions.** The licence granted in Section 3 above is expressly made subject to and limited by the following restrictions:
   a You may distribute, publicly display, publicly perform, or publicly digitally perform the Work only under the terms of this Licence, and You must include a copy of, or the Uniform Resource Identifier for, this Licence with every copy or phonorecord of the Work You distribute, publicly display, publicly perform, or publicly digitally perform. You may not offer or impose any terms on the Work that alter or restrict the terms of this Licence or the recipients' exercise of the rights granted hereunder. You may not sublicence the Work. You must keep intact all notices that refer to this Licence and to the disclaimer of warranties. You may not distribute, publicly display, publicly perform, or publicly digitally perform the Work with any technological measures that control access or use of the Work in a manner inconsistent with the terms of this Licence Agreement. The above applies to the Work as incorporated in a Collective Work, but this does not require the Collective Work apart from the Work itself to be made subject to the terms of this Licence. If You create a Collective Work, upon notice from any Licencor You must, to the extent practicable, remove from the Collective Work any reference to such Licensor or the Original Author, as requested.
   b You may not exercise any of the rights granted to You in Section 3 above in any manner that is primarily intended for or directed toward commercial advantage or private monetary

compensation. The exchange of the Work for other copyrighted works by means of digital file-sharing or otherwise shall not be considered to be intended for or directed toward commercial advantage or private monetary compensation, provided there is no payment of any monetary compensation in connection with the exchange of copyrighted works.

c If you distribute, publicly display, publicly perform, or publicly digitally perform the Work or any Collective Works, You must keep intact all copyright notices for the Work and give the Original Author credit reasonable to the medium or means You are utilizing by conveying the name (or pseudonym if applicable) of the Original Author if supplied; the title of the Work if supplied. Such credit may be implemented in any reasonable manner; provided, however, that in the case of a Collective Work, at a minimum such credit will appear where any other comparable authorship credit appears and in a manner at least as prominent as such other comparable authorship credit.

5. Representations, Warranties and Disclaimer

   a By offering the Work for public release under this Licence, Licensor represents and warrants that, to the best of Licensor's knowledge after reasonable inquiry:

      i Licensor has secured all rights in the Work necessary to grant the licence rights hereunder and to permit the lawful exercise of the rights granted hereunder without You having any obligation to pay any royalties, compulsory licence fees, residuals or any other payments;

      ii The Work does not infringe the copyright, trademark, publicity rights, common law rights or any other right of any third party or constitute defamation, invasion of privacy or other tortious injury to any third party.

   b EXCEPT AS EXPRESSLY STATED IN THIS LICENCE OR OTHERWISE AGREED IN WRITING OR REQUIRED BY APPLICABLE LAW, THE WORK IS LICENCED ON AN "AS IS" BASIS, WITHOUT WARRANTIES OF ANY KIND, EITHER EXPRESS OR IMPLIED INCLUDING, WITHOUT LIMITATION, ANY WARRANTIES REGARDING THE CONTENTS OR ACCURACY OF THE WORK.

6. Limitation on Liability. EXCEPT TO THE EXTENT REQUIRED BY APPLICABLE LAW, AND EXCEPT FOR DAMAGES ARISING FROM LIABILITY TO A THIRD PARTY RESULTING FROM BREACH OF THE WARRANTIES IN SECTION 5, IN NO EVENT WILL LICENSOR BE LIABLE TO YOU ON ANY LEGAL THEORY FOR ANY SPECIAL, INCIDENTAL, CONSEQUENTIAL, PUNITIVE OR EXEMPLARY DAMAGES ARISING OUT OF THIS LICENCE OR THE USE OF THE WORK, EVEN IF LICENSOR HAS BEEN ADVISED OF THE POSSIBILITY OF SUCH DAMAGES.

7. Termination

   a This Licence and the rights granted hereunder will terminate automatically upon any breach by You of the terms of this Licence. Individuals or entities who have received Collective Works from You under this Licence, however, will not have their licences terminated provided such individuals or entities remain in full compliance with those licences. Sections 1, 2, 5, 6, 7, and 8 will survive any termination of this Licence.

   b Subject to the above terms and conditions, the licence granted here is perpetual (for the duration of the applicable copyright in the Work). Notwithstanding the above, Licensor reserves the right to release the Work under different licence terms or to stop distributing the Work at any time; provided, however that any such election will not serve to withdraw this Licence (or any other licence that has been, or is required to be, granted under the terms of this Licence), and this Licence will continue in full force and effect unless terminated as stated above.

8. Miscellaneous

   a Each time You distribute or publicly digitally perform the Work or a Collective Work, DEMOS offers to the recipient a licence to the Work on the same terms and conditions as the licence granted to You under this Licence.

   b If any provision of this Licence is invalid or unenforceable under applicable law, it shall not affect the validity or enforceability of the remainder of the terms of this Licence, and without further action by the parties to this agreement, such provision shall be reformed to the minimum extent necessary to make such provision valid and enforceable.

   c No term or provision of this Licence shall be deemed waived and no breach consented to unless such waiver or consent shall be in writing and signed by the party to be charged with such waiver or consent.

   d This Licence constitutes the entire agreement between the parties with respect to the Work licensed here. There are no understandings, agreements or representations with respect to the Work not specified here. Licensor shall not be bound by any additional provisions that may appear in any communication from You. This Licence may not be modified without the mutual written agreement of DEMOS and You.